Making Thirteen Colonies

A   H I S T O R Y   O F   U S

The picture on the cover is a detail from an oil painting by Edward Hicks (1780-1849). It is called *Penn's Treaty with the Indians*; it shows William Penn and other Quakers making a peace treaty with the Indians of Pennsylvania. (To see the whole painting, turn to page 108.) Hicks was a sign painter and a Quaker preacher who began painting pictures late in life. His work became very popular. Sometimes he wrote poems and painted them around the edges of his compositions.

Oxford University Press

A HISTORY
OF
US

BOOK TWO

Making Thirteen Colonies

Joy Hakim

Oxford University Press
New York

Oxford University Press

Oxford   New York

Auckland   Bangkok   Buenos Aires
Cape Town   Chennai   Dar es Salaam   Delhi   Hong Kong   Istanbul
Karachi   Kolkata   Kuala Lumpur   Madrid   Melbourne   Mexico City   Mumbai
Nairobi   São Paulo   Shanghai   Taipei   Tokyo   Toronto

Third Edition

Published by Oxford University Press, Inc.,
198 Madison Avenue, New York, New York 10016
Oxford is a registered trademark of Oxford University Press

Library of Congress Cataloging-in-Publication Data is available

ISBN 0-19-515321-9 (cloth)
ISBN 978-0-19-515322-4 (paper)
ISBN 0-19-515322-7 (paper)

9 8
Printed in the United States of America on acid-free paper

THIS BOOK IS FOR NATALIE JOHNSON, WHO SKIS, RUNS TRACK,
CARES ABOUT PEOPLE, AND WRITES POETRY.

This engraving was done by Theodore de Bry in 1618. It is entitled "Employment for Gentlemen in New England."

Thomas Morton, an Englishman, who landed in America in 1622, was full of optimism and good cheer. He liked what he saw. This is what he wrote:

In the month of June 1622, it was my chance to arrive in the parts of New England. . . While our houses were building, I did endeavor to take a survey of the country. The more I looked, the more I liked it. And when I had more seriously considered of the beauty of the place, with all her fair endowments, I did not think that in all the known world it could be paralleled. . . in my eye 'twas nature's Masterpiece. . .

But to William Bradford, who came that same year, the land didn't look promising. Here are his thoughts:

Besides, what could they see but a hideous and desolate wilderness, full of wild beasts and wild men? And what multitudes there might be of them they knew not. . . for which way soever they turned their eye, they could have little solace (comfort). . . For summer being done, all things stand upon them with a weather-beaten face; and the whole country represented a wild and savage [way].

Contents

Puritan colonist

*Metacom, or King Philip of
the Wampanoag people*

An animal which has a head like a sucking pig...hair like a badger...the tail like a rat, the paws like a monkey, which has a purse beneath its belly, where it produces its young and nourishes them.

—LE MOYNE D'IBERVILLE, WRITING IN 1699 IN ASTONISHMENT AT AN OPOSSUM, AN ANIMAL UNKNOWN IN EUROPE

Some ten years ago being in Virginia, and taken prisoner by the power of Powhatan their chief King, I received from this great savage exceeding great courtesy, especially from his son Nantaquaua, the most manliest, comeliest, boldest spirit I ever saw in a savage, and his sister Pocahontas, the King's most dear and well beloved daughter, being but a child of 12 or 13 years of age, whose compassionate pitiful heart, of my desperate state, gave me much cause to respect her.... Jamestown she as frequently visited as her father's habitation; and during the time of two or three years, she next under God, was still the instrument to preserve this Colony from death, famine and utter confusion.

—JOHN SMITH, ADVENTURER AND CO-FOUNDER OF JAMESTOWN, VIRGINIA

Ætatis suæ 21. Aᵒ. 1616.

...toaks als Rebecka daughter to the mighty Prince ...whatan Emperour of Attanoughkomouck als Virginia ...verted and baptized in the Christian faith, and ...Wife to the worᵗ Mʳ Tho: Rolff.

PREFACE
Our Mixed-Up Civilization

Carved 4,000 years ago, this is the portrait of a man who ruled in Sumer around the time Abraham lived.

A long time ago—actually, it was about 4,000 years ago—in the city of Ur, there lived a boy named Abraham. Ur was in a country that is now known as Iraq but was then called Sumer.

Now you may be asking why we are in ancient Sumer when this is a book about U.S. history. Well, hold on. Abraham's story will turn out to be important—to people all over the world—and to us in America.

Abraham lived in an interesting urban center. In Sumer, between the Tigris (TY-griss) and Euphrates (yoo-FRAY-teez) rivers, people had learned to read and write and to build and govern cities (which hadn't been done much before). But something must have been wrong, because one day Abraham and his father decided to move.

Abraham moved with his whole family and his cattle and oxen. He traveled northwest, following a fingernail of green land called the Fertile Crescent. He went to a place known as Canaan (KAY-nun); he called it the land of Israel. There Abraham had two sons: Isaac and Ishmael. The descendants of those sons founded two great religions. From Isaac's children came Judaism and the Jewish people; from Ishmael's came Islam and the Muslims.

Abraham must have been a restless type, because he traveled on, to Egypt and back to Canaan. In Egypt he found a spectacular civilization, where people could also read and write. The Egyptians had built big cities and tall pyramids. They called their rulers *pharaohs* (FAIR-oze), and they kept slaves—as did many people in those days. Some of Abraham's people became slaves. Like all enslaved people, they longed to be free. Help was on its way.

This preface is a synopsis (sin OP sis; it means a brief retelling) of some ancient history. It includes stories of people from the Bible. Are they history? Many historians would say "no." We can't document those stories. But they were so widely told and believed that they influenced world history. You can't understand history if you don't know people's stories and beliefs.

Ancient Sumer
is sometimes called
Sumeria or Mesopotamia.

According to the biblical story, the pharaoh's daughter finds Moses. Her clothes, and her castle, don't look very ancient Egyptian. When this illustration was made, in the 15th century, artists just drew people the way they looked in their own time.

A Greek painted this vase 2,500 years ago with a scene from the *Iliad:* the Greeks and Trojans fight over the fallen body of the Greek hero Achilles *(in the middle).*

One day an Egyptian princess found a baby boy floating in a basket among the bulrushes at the edge of the river Nile. The baby was Moses. He became a great leader and led the Jewish people out of Egypt. The trip was filled with danger and adventure. It took Moses and the Jews 40 years to get to their destination: Israel. Actually, Moses didn't quite make it. You can read the story of that flight to freedom in the Hebrew Bible, which is also called the Old Testament.

Take a look at the map on page 181. Do you see Israel and Egypt? Did you notice that they are next to the Mediterranean Sea? Back in the old, old days, before cars, buses, trains, and airplanes, it was very hard traveling over land. It was much easier to get in a boat and sail away. So people who lived near the sea got around more than inland people. People living around the Mediterranean Sea traveled and traded ideas.

Greece borders the Mediterranean. More than 2,500 years ago, some very interesting people—artists, playwrights, scientists, and philosophers—lived in Greece. The most renowned Greek of those long-ago days was a blind man who had been a slave. His name was Homer and he was a poet and a storyteller. Homer's stories were so good that we still read them today. They are stories of real heroes and heroines and of mythological gods and goddesses. Homer's two adventure books, the *Iliad* and the *Odyssey,* are among the best books ever written.

The Greeks had an idea for governing people that hadn't been tried before. They called it "democracy." In the Greek language, *democracy* means "people's rule." In Athens, which was a powerful city-state, the Greeks tried democracy. They let the people (except for women, slaves, and non-Greeks) vote and rule themselves. The idea (remarkable at the time) was that the state existed for its citizens. Solon (638-559 BCE), an Athenian leader, decreed that every citizen, rich or poor, was to be equal before the law. Athens flourished; commerce thrived, as did art, music, poetry and science. But some philosophers (deep thinkers), believing that majority rule led to mob rule, spoke out and criticized the democracy. Their ideas weren't popular; many thought them dangerous. The citizen-voters decided to kill Socrates (SOCK ruh teez), the greatest of the philosophers. That made Socrates' student, Plato (429-347 BCE), think deeply about how people should be educated and governed. He wrote a book, called *The Republic*. In it he said that the wisest citizens (including women) should be trained to rule for the benefit of all. (Do you agree?) Some of Plato's ideas are disturbing; like the best writers, he makes you think.

The Romans were a different Mediterranean people. They spoke Latin. Power was held by the wealthy and aristocratic. Then in 509 BCE, the plebeians (ordinary working people) rebelled. They created a republic: a government where people elect representatives who govern according to law. In 458 BCE, Rome was under attack. Lucius Quinctius Cincinnatus left his farm to become dictator, lead an army, and save the city. Sixteen days later he gave up his power and went back to his farm. (That's a story that inspired our George Washington.) Later, another Roman general, Julius Caesar (100-44 BCE), became dictator; he conquered the Mediterranean world and much of Europe. The Romans built roads, fielded a strong army, and mostly brought stability and peace to the lands they dominated. A Roman named Virgil (70-19 BCE) took Homer's stories and other tales and put them in a book called the *Aeneid* (uh NEE id) that is still good to read. (The men who wrote our Constitution wanted a republic; they looked to Rome for ideas.)

Rome was ruling most of the Mediterranean lands when a Jewish boy, named Jesus, was born in Israel. Jesus lived in a town called Nazareth. From his preaching and his example a great new religion grew. That religion was Christianity. The ideas of Jesus are written in the New Testament. Jesus Christ was born about the year 1. Modern history dates from the birth of Christ.

Another child was born in the land to the east of the Mediterranean. He was Mohammed, a descendant of Ishmael, and he was born in the city of Mecca in the year 570. Look at a map on page 13 and find Mecca. Mohammed founded the religion known as Islam, and his teachings are found in a book called the Koran. People who practice Islam are known as Mohammedans or Muslims.

Islam spread rapidly across Arabian lands and into North Africa and the Sudan (often through religious warfare). In the year 711 an African general, Taril ibn Ziyad, sailed an army 13 miles from

Pericles was a great Greek general and statesman. This is what he said in 431 BCE, "Our constitution does not copy the laws of neighboring states; we are rather a pattern to others than imitators ourselves. Its administration favors the many instead of the few; this is why it is called a democracy."

In 1947, an Arab herdsman was grazing his flock near the Dead Sea in Jordan. He went after a stray goat and stumbled into a cave, which contained some old, old jars and baskets. In them, wrapped in linen, were ancient scrolls, written in Hebrew, in Greek, and in Aramaic, an ancient language related to Hebrew and Arabic. Later more caves and scrolls were found. The Dead Sea Scrolls are the oldest known copies of parts of the Hebrew Bible; they may have been written before the birth of Christ.

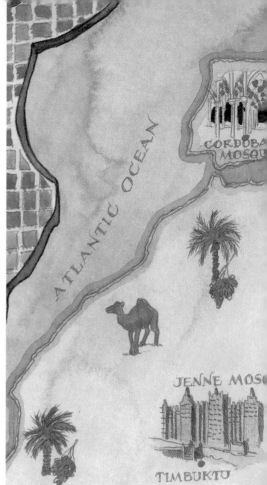

In a feudal system, the peasants have to declare their loyalty to a lord and do a certain amount of work for him. In return, the lord is supposed to protect the workers and help them in bad times. Working for a lord like this was a bit better than being a slave, but not much.

Monks are men who gave up worldly goods and entered a monastery, a place where they devote their lives to religion. In the Middle Ages monasteries were big and powerful. They had their own farms, workshops, and schools, and usually didn't have to buy anything from outside.

Caravels were ships first built in the 15th century. They made long voyages possible, because they could sail into the wind.

Morocco across the mouth of the Mediterranean Sea and landed on a Spanish hill. That rocky hill became known as Jabal Taril (Taril's hill), which was soon shortened to Gibraltar.

Taril's army of Muslim Africans fought and defeated an army led by King Rodrigo of Spain. For the next seven and a half centuries much of Spain was ruled by Muslims (the Spaniards called them Moors). It was a splendid era in Spain. It was a time of religious tolerance: Jews, Muslims, and Christians lived together in harmony. The Moors built great cities with centers of learning. Agriculture flourished in Spain as it never had before or has since. These were the Middle Ages, so called because they lie between ancient days and modern times. In the Middle Ages, most Europeans were Roman Catholic Christians.

It was a time when knights, lords, and ladies lived in splendid feudal castles. And religious crusaders set off for Israel to recapture the Holy Land from the Muslims. Some managed to plunder and murder as they went.

Most people weren't lords or knights, and most didn't go on crusades. Most were peasants. They worked on the land, and their lives were short and hard. They couldn't read, they didn't get a chance to travel, and they didn't know much. Books were kept in monasteries and were read only by monks. Most Europeans had forgotten the arts and learning of the Greeks and Romans.

It was different in Spain. Remember, Arabs, Jews, and Christians had brought their scholarship, arts, and energy to that land. Spain was thriving. Then the Moors started fighting among themselves. Christian armies soon entered the fray. By 1250, Muslims controlled only one Spanish region, Granada. When they lost that in 1492, Christian kings and armies held Spain. Jews had to convert or

THE MEDITERRANEAN WORLD

leave the country immediately. The Moors were also thrown out, but more gradually.

Meanwhile, in the places that would become France, England, Germany, and Italy, cities were growing and trade was expanding. The Middle Ages were being replaced by a Renaissance (REN-uh-sahnce)—a rebirth of learning and art. It was the forgotten ideas of the ancient Greeks and Romans that were being reborn. The Renaissance began in Italy and soon was inspiring thinkers all through Europe. At the same time, travelers were describing the fabulous civilizations in the Far East. Before people could even digest all the fresh ideas, two whole new continents—South and North America—were discovered. And seagoing explorers proved, beyond anyone's doubt, that the world was round. As if that weren't enough, the Catholic Church was rocked by reformers (people who wanted to change the Church); that led to a host of new Christian Churches, called "Protestant." At the same time, the European nations (that we know today) were being formed. As you can see, it was an exciting time, but confusing, too.

The ideas of all these peoples—with all their religions and cul-

Marco Polo, a trader from Venice, went to China in the years 1275–1292. He saw wonderful things, met the Grand Khan, and came back and wrote a book about it all.

This sign was the Totem of the Five Nations. In 1570, five Indian tribes, the Oneida, Mohawk, Cayuga, Seneca, and Onondaga, united in an Iroquois confederation.

A Great Mystery

A Dakota Indian named Luther Standing Bear thought about the meeting of Native Americans and Europeans and wrote: While the white people had much to teach us, we had much to teach them, and what a school could have been established upon that idea!...Only the white man saw nature as a "wilderness," and only to him was the land "infested" with "wild" animals and savage people. To us it was tame. Earth was bountiful and we were surrounded with the blessings of the Great Mystery.

tures—made up an idea pool, a kind of cultural stew, that sailed to America across the ocean from Europe. (Both the good ideas and the bad came to America. One bad idea was slavery. Some of all the peoples we have talked about kept slaves.)

In America there were already civilizations as ancient as those that had begun in Ur and Egypt and Greece. The Indian civilizations surprised the Europeans. To begin with, they weren't all alike. Some Native Americans were ruled by powerful lords. Some practiced slavery. But others lived democratically. The Iroquois had a government of the people. Women were important in Iroquois society, and there was much freedom.

There were no democracies in Europe. Mostly there were kings and emperors. Many of the European newcomers were impressed with the free life the Indians led. They thought about that free life and added it to their idea pool.

Unfortunately, many of the newcomers didn't understand the Native American cultures. Because they were different, the Europeans thought them inferior. They called the Indians "savages."They destroyed much of the Indian heritage before they came to appreciate it.

The European newcomers learned more from the Native Americans than they realized. They learned ways of planting, harvesting, and hunting. They added Indian words to their languages. They exchanged foods, animals, diseases, and even weeds. Indian ways enriched the new culture that was forming. That culture became a mixture: Africans came—in chains—but that didn't stop them from adding ideas, energy, stories, music, and knowledge of agriculture. Then people came from Asia, bringing the wisdom of ancient religions and cultures.

Out of that worldwide mixture a nation developed—our nation, the United States—and a new civilization, an American civilization, where peoples of East and West and of many races and religions now live together and share ideas.

What does that mixing do for us? It makes life in the United States very interesting. People in America eat pizza, chow mein, and pita bread—sometimes in the same meal. In America, children whose ancestors left England in tiny wooden boats go to school with children who themselves left Vietnam in tiny wooden boats. In America, children who worship in a church go to school with children who worship in a mosque or temple or synagogue or kiva. In America, people who have their own beliefs—rather than those of an organized religion—are given respect.

Our nation began as an experiment. Nothing like it had ever been tried before. The citizens of most other countries couldn't even imagine living with people who seemed different from them. Can people who don't look alike build a free and equal society together? Read on, and see for yourself.

1 A Sign in the Sky

Experts disagree about whether Halley's was the comet seen in 1066. Some say it was; others say it may not have been the same comet.

A Comet's Blaze

In 1607 a dazzling comet lit the sky over Europe. "A comet, a comet!" people cried and pointed to the heavens. In those days almost everyone could name the bright stars and planets. They knew the constellations and the mythical stories of their forming. Mothers and fathers showed their children the stars named for the dog Sirius, or Draco the Dragon, or Cygnus the Swan.

Pollution and city lights had not yet dimmed the skies. Nor was there much else in the evening to capture attention. Few could afford costly candles. So when something out of the ordinary appeared in the night sky, people saw it and wondered at its meaning.

These were times when most questions were answered by religious faith or superstition. Modern science was just being born. Stars were thought to be the lights of heaven, and comets were said to be messengers sent to foretell danger and dire change.

Many who watched the bold comet were frightened. They might have been even more fearful had they known this was the very comet that had been seen in 1066, when the Norman kings invaded England from France. Those French conquerors had changed England, and the English language, for all time.

But you didn't need a comet in 1607 to see that Europe was changing. The old religion—Catholic Christianity—had broken apart. England had become Protestant, then Catholic, then Protestant again. Now some people, called Puritans, were saying that the country wasn't Protestant enough. It was all very disturbing to people used to a secure faith. To make matters worse, there were economic problems, too.

In the great Catholic nation of Spain, the government was bankrupt. Although nobody knew it, Spain's glory days were over. Would

This is a diagram from Copernicus's *On the Revolution of the Celestial Spheres*. It was the first time ever (1543) that the sun *(Sol)* was shown at the center of the solar system.

Even when Galileo was made to recant (deny) his belief that the earth moved around the sun, he didn't really deny it. Afterward, it is said, he muttered quietly, "And yet, it moves."

Galileo (pictured above and on the opposite page) was disgraced by the Catholic Church and put under house arrest for saying that the earth moves around the sun. Galileo was lucky. The great scholar Giordano Bruno (1548–1600) was burned alive by Italian authorities when he said that the universe was infinite. Yet by the end of the 17th century, most of the new scientific beliefs about the earth and skies were commonly accepted.

that arrogant little Protestant island—that England—become Europe's new leader? Now that England's magnificent Queen Elizabeth was dead, no one knew where England was heading.

In this world that had once seemed orderly, ideas were changing. New thinkers, like the Italian scientist Galileo Galilei, were actually saying that Aristotle, the greatest of scientists, had some ideas that were wrong! Galileo even whispered that Nicholas Copernicus might be right. Copernicus, a Polish astronomer, had said the sun, not the earth, was the center of our universe. How could that be? Everyone knew that the planets and stars and sun all revolved around the earth. If that idea was wrong then the Pope and all of Europe's rulers were wrong.

Of course, that disturbing idea got Galileo into a lot of trouble. It ended up changing everything people believed. Change is troublesome, especially to those in power. And yet the new ideas, like germs, seemed to travel on invisible wings. The epidemic of thought was soon out of control.

In 1609, just two years after the comet appeared, Galileo built one of the world's first telescopes. (It was a lot stronger and therefore more useful than the few made before it.) Galileo took much of the mystery from the skies and replaced it with scientific order. When the comet of 1607 came again, in 1682, an English scientist named Edmond Halley tracked it and learned that it takes more than 75 years to complete its trips around the sun. Halley predicted that the comet would return in 1758, and he was right.

But in 1607 people knew none of that. They didn't know the year 1607 was to become famous. That very year the seeds of a new nation—a new way of governing, a new way of looking at the world—were being planted on the North American continent by a small group of English men and boys.

The message that some people read in the comet was right: the world was in for astonishing changes. Would they be changes for the better? Not for those people called Indians, who would soon meet the pale-skinned English. For them the changes were tragic.

But for England, and the rest of the world, 1607 marked the beginning of what turned out to be an awesome, momentous, earth-shaking experiment. An experiment that would lead to democracy and to a government dedicated to liberty and the pursuit of happiness.

Let's watch the United States happen. Take yourself to the beginning of the 17th century, to England, where some brave men are getting ready to travel to a place they call the New World. They have no idea what is ahead of them. They'll bring along their Old World ideas—good and bad. Pack a bag, we're going to join them.

Diagram labels: NEPTUNE · ORBIT of URANUS · ORBIT of SATURN · EARTH · SUN · MERCURY · VENUS · HALLEY'S COMET · EARTH · ORBIT of MARS · HALLEY'S COMET · ORBIT of JUPITER

You don't need Galileo's telescope to see Halley's comet. It's the only comet that passes close enough to earth to be seen easily with the naked eye. It has been observed 30 times since 467 B.C.E. *Above:* Halley's orbit through our solar system in 1985, its most recent visit. At the far end of its path, away from the sun, the comet goes outside the orbit of Neptune. It will be back in 2061.

· Galileo Galilei ·

17

2 Across the Ocean

English ships of the 17th century were sturdy but tiny. An ocean voyage in one seemed endless.

To *embark* means to "set off."

On the docks of the river Thames (TEMS), near London, a group of Englishmen readied themselves for a trip across the vast ocean. They were brave men, as they had to be to embark on an adventure such as they had in mind. They were going to a New World, where there were strange animals, deep forests, and people said to be wild.

There was also gold. They were sure of that. A play, popular in London, told of Virginia. It said:

> I tell thee, gold is more plentiful there than copper is with us.... Why, man, all their dripping pans and their chamber pots are pure gold...and as for rubies and diamonds, they go forth on holy days and gather them by the seashore, to hang on their children's coats and stick in their caps.

Of course the authors of that play had never been to Virginia, but people believed them. Everyone knew there was gold in America. Hadn't the Spaniards found mountains of gold? And wasn't England now the greatest of nations? Her time had come.

About 144 men actually set sail for America, but the sailors weren't counted because they returned to England.

Of the 105 men who stood on the docks, more than half listed themselves as "gentlemen". In England, gentlemen were not expected or trained to work. They lived on family money. They had time for adventure; they hoped to find riches.

Most brought their best clothes for the trip: their puffed knee pants, their silk stockings, their feathered hats, their gaudy blouses.

Gaudy means "showy and brightly colored."

Those in plainer clothes were the gentlemen's servants; a few were carpenters and bricklayers; four of them were boys—probably orphans or runaways. The boys were called "younkers" and were ex-

18

In dirty, crowded London it was easy to imagine that America was an untouched Garden of Eden. It had to be full of animals known to Europeans only from myths—but which most people firmly believed existed somewhere.

A *peril* is a danger or risk. A *privateer* was a pirate with a government license. Privateers split their loot with the king.

pected to climb the rigging, high on the ship's mast, help set the sails, and keep a lookout for land and danger. If a younker fell in the ocean and was lost—well, too bad. That was one of the perils of sea travel.

Ocean travel was risky—they all knew that. They also knew that their captain, Christopher Newport, was one of England's finest sailors. As a privateer, he had sailed the New World's seas. Queen Elizabeth had encouraged English captains to prey on Spanish ships. And Newport had led an expedition that destroyed or captured 20 Spanish vessels and sacked four towns in the West Indies and Florida. He was an English hero. What the Spaniards thought of him is something else.

But the men and boys who climbed onto three small ships and set sail down the river Thames felt confident with Newport in command. What surprised them all were contrary winds.

They sailed into the Atlantic, and the winds blew them back to England. Out they went again—and back. For six weeks those strange winds blew, while the voyagers ate their precious food and got nowhere. Now there were grumblings. Some wished they'd never come. Do you think they were scared? Do you think they thought of turning back? Pretend you are a younker. Are you excited? Or afraid? Or both?

Short Rations

The ships of the day were brightly painted with striped masts, banners, and flags. But there was never really enough food aboard for the six- or eight-week voyage. Those who made it across were usually weak and hungry when they landed—if not dead or sick with scurvy. A sailor's song went like this:

We ate the mice, we ate the rats,

And through the hold we ran like cats.

This is supposed to be a three-toed sloth. The artist had probably never been to America, let alone seen a sloth, so he made up an idea of it from someone else's description.

Abundance means "plenty."

Ballast is a heavy substance carried in a boat to make it more stable in rolling seas. ("Ballast" is a good word to know; a dictionary will give you additional meanings.) The early ships that sailed to America carried soil as ballast. When they arrived in America, sailors dumped the ballast to make room for "New World" cargo. Scientists are now studying the long-term effects of that introduction of foreign beetles, worms, and bacteria into the American ecosystem. (What's an ecosystem?)

They had boarded ship in December 1606, but it was February of 1607 when, finally, they lost sight of England. Captain Newport soon had them in the Canary Islands, where the three ships took on fresh water and food. Then they were off to the islands of the West Indies, where they rested and prepared themselves.

For they understood, when they left the West Indian island of Martinique, that they were heading for little-known territory. They were to do something Englishmen had not done before: they were to start a colony on the mainland. Spain had grown rich because of her colonies. England would beat Spain at that game. These Englishmen were determined to enrich England—and themselves, too.

For a few of the voyagers there may have been something else besides gold that drew them to America: that was its beauty and abundance. Those who had seen the land wrote of birds and flowers and fish more gorgeous than one could imagine. A poet called Virginia "earth's only Paradise."

England seemed crowded. Timber was scarce and getting scarcer. Farmland was disappearing. London's streets were filled with beggars.

Might America's land and trees and soil be as valuable as the gold nuggets the adventurers thought they were sure to find? Could this New World become a land of hope and opportunity? There were some in England who thought so.

The colonists were certainly headed for a new life in Virginia—but not always a good one. Fliers like these were put out to attract more settlers. Sometimes they weren't very truthful.

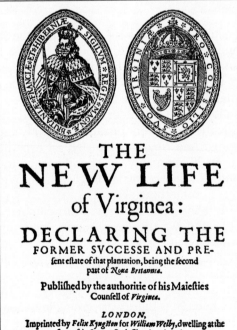

THE
NEW LIFE
of Virginea:
DECLARING THE
FORMER SVCCESSE AND PRE-
sent estate of that plantation, being the second
part of *Nova Britannia*.

Published by the authoritie of his Maiesties
Counsell of *Virginea*.

LONDON,
Imprinted by *Felix Kyngston* for *William Welby*, dwelling at the
signe of the Swan in Pauls Churchyard. 1612.

3 The First Virginians

The Powhatan had about 9,000 subjects; his land stretched from what is now Washington, D.C., to northern North Carolina.

When English parents told stories to their children, they often spoke of monsters, trolls, wild beasts, and witches. Those were savage stories, strange and disturbing. Since everyone knew there was a savage side to life, the stories had a kind of realness to them, even when they were make-believe.

But those weren't the only stories they told. There were tales of splendor and goodness, too. Every child heard the Bible's first story, which is of a Garden of Eden. Eden was a place of great beauty, a paradise. Many of the goodness stories were about sweet, simple people who lived in harmony with nature. And those stories seemed real, too, because there was much goodness in the world.

Did you know that the stories you read in childhood stay with you all your life? They influence adults more than most of them realize. So when English men and women learned of a land of great beauty, where people lived close to nature, many of the English thought of that land as paradise. They called the natives "savages," but meant the word kindly. The first English visitors to the New World described the Indians as "courteous" and "gentle" and "great."

But, later, when others met those great savages, they found they didn't always act as people do in storybooks. Soon some were calling them worse names than "savages." They called them "beasts." Some said they were servants of the devil. Others said they were part animal and part human.

But those people—the Indians—were just real people, like the English. They lived in families, in towns, governed by leaders. They farmed, hunted, played games, and fashioned beautiful objects.

Earthly Paradise

We have discovered... the goodliest soil under the cope of heaven, so abounding with sweet trees, that bring such sundry rich and pleasant gums, grapes of such greatness, as France, Spain, nor Italy have no greater....the continent is of huge and unknown greatness, and very well peopled and towned, though savagely, and the climate so wholesome, that we had not one sick since we landed here.

It was letters like this one, written by Ralph Lane in 1585, that made people want to go to the New World. Lane was a member of Raleigh's Roanoke Colony.

21

An *estuary* (ESS-tew-air-ee) is the body of water where the mouth of a river meets the sea.

The bear grease that the Indians rubbed on their bodies made their brown skin shine with a reddish glow. Europeans thought it really was red, and that was how the name "redskin," which many Europeans once used for Native Americans, came to be. It's based on a *misperception*, which is an error in the way things are seen.

Remember, horses first came to America with the Spanish conquistadors. Even 100 years later they were still a rarity.

Some of them were wise and some were foolish. Some were kind and some were mean. But most were a bit of all those things.

One of the most interesting Indians the English would meet was the Powhatan, the ruler or emperor of eastern Virginia. His real name was Wahunsonacock, and he had inherited an empire of five tribes. Through daring, strength and leadership, Powhatan soon held sway over dozens of villages and thousands of Indians. The English would call the Indians of his empire Powhatan Indians.

They were Woodland Indians, who spoke Algonquian (al-GON-kwee-un) dialects and hunted, fished, and farmed in a region of great abundance. The area surrounded the Chesapeake Bay and went west to mountain foothills and south to what would someday be North Carolina's border. It was a land of rivers, bays, and estuaries; of ducks, geese, wild turkeys, and deer; of fertile soil, fish, and shellfish; of wild berries, nuts, and grapes.

Powhatan's people raised vegetables—corn, beans, squash, and pumpkins—which was more than half the food they ate. Because they farmed, they lived in settled villages. Corn was their most important food. They ground it and made it into flat pancakes that served as bread or rice does in many other cultures. Aside from corn, the food they ate changed with the seasons: fresh vegetables in summer and fall; game in winter; and fish, stored nuts, and berries in the spring. (Spring was when corn supplies ran low and they sometimes went hungry.)

There was much small game in the region: raccoon, opossum, squirrel, turkey, and rabbit. But it was deer these Indians relied on most for food and clothing. Unfortunately, like people elsewhere, they overhunted; deer became scarce. And they knew if they roamed outside the Powhatan's territory—looking for better hunting grounds—they risked war with other tribes.

It was the men who hunted, fished, and fought. Women farmed. Men and women had set roles in this society and rarely changed them. Children helped their parents, played, and didn't go to work until they were young adults.

The boys often played in scarecrow houses that stood in the middle of the fields. From there they threw stones at rabbits or other animals that might nibble on the crops. It trained their throwing arms, and that helped when they became hunters. Little girls played with clay, made pots, and helped their mothers plant and cook. Boys and girls played running games. There were no horses (they hadn't arrived in this part of the New World yet), so fast runners were prized. Sometimes they would dress up like their parents—painting their bodies and wearing necklaces and bracelets of shells and beads and animal bones.

Men and women tattooed beautiful designs all over their bodies. Men sometimes hung animal claws, birds' wings, bats, even live green snakes around their necks. They rubbed themselves with bear grease—it repelled mosquitoes, kept them warm, and made their skin glisten in the sunshine. Most of the year these Indians needed little clothing, although in winter they wore deerskin garments and, sometimes, cloaks of feathers or fur.

Captain John Smith would never have been able to make this map of Virginia without help from the local Algonquian Indians, the Powhatans. You'll hear more about John Smith in Chapter 5.

23

Werowance is a Delaware Indian word that means, literally, "he is rich."

Powhatan was said to have 100 wives. One-third of his 9,000 subjects were warriors. Powhatan gave his decorated deerskin to Captain Christopher Newport. It is now in a museum in Oxford, England.

The Chesapeakes lived on land that is now included in the cities of Virginia Beach, Norfolk, Portsmouth, and Chesapeake.

The great Powhatan had a beautiful deerskin sewed with designs in lustrous pearls. Powhatan had stacks of deerskins and a storehouse of corn, and he had copper and pearls. The tribes brought all this and more to him. It was tribute given to a ruler.

Each tribe had its own leader, called a *werowance* (WEER-ah-wunts), and also priests and healers and others with power. But the Powhatan was special. All those who met him noted it. He knew how to command, when to be stern and unforgiving and when to be understanding. The story was told of the time he visited the Potomacs (puh-TOW-mucks), who were under his rule. The young Potomac warriors came before him, and each told of awesome deeds of valor against fierce enemies or wild beasts of the forest.

Finally one young man stood before Powhatan and said, "I, my lord, went this morning into the woods and valiantly killed six muskrats. While that may be no more than boys do, it is true, while much you have heard is fable." When Powhatan heard that, he broke into laughter and gave a reward to the truth teller.

Powhatan's priests had foretold that his mighty empire would one day be destroyed by men from the east. The Chesapeakes, who lived by the ocean, were the easternmost of his tribes. Perhaps that is why, just before the 16th century turned into the 17th (in the European method of reckoning), Powhatan fought the mighty Chesapeake Indians and left them weak and powerless.

Powhatan didn't yet know that three small ships were heading for his realm. They were coming across the ocean from an island far to the east.

Virginian Indians cooking a stew of corn, fish, and beans. This picture was drawn at the end of the 16th century by John White.

4 English Settlers Come to Stay

The crown and coat of arms on the Virginia Company's seal show that it was granted by the king.

In Virginia, April is a sweet month. Strawberries and white dogwoods blossom below the green of tall pines. Redbuds are emerging, and so are grape leaves, honeysuckle, and wild roses.

It was thus in April of 1607, when three small ships landed at the mouth of the Chesapeake Bay. The ships were the *Susan Constant,* the *Discovery,* and the *Godspeed*, and they had been sent from England by a business corporation called the London Company.

They were the same three ships that left the docks on the river Thames. The voyagers had been told to look for gold and a river or passage that would go through the country to China and Japan. They were also to see if there were other ways to make money on this unknown continent.

The ships anchored near an elbow of beach they named Cape Henry (in honor of young Henry, the king's oldest son). Some of the mariners rowed to shore and set out exploring. "We could find nothing worth the speaking of, but fair meadows and goodly tall trees, with such fresh waters running through the woods, as I was almost ravished at the first sight thereof," wrote George Percy, who was one of the gentlemen adventurers.

On their way back to the ship the Englishmen were attacked by Indians, who came "creeping upon all fours…like bears, with their bows in their mouths," but when "they felt the sharpness of our shot, they retired into the woods with a great noise."

The local Indians knew about white men, and they didn't want them around. Spain—England's old enemy—had tried to start two colonies in the Chesapeake Bay area. An Indian prince from the re-

From the instructions of the London Company to the First Settlers: "When it shall please God to Send you on the Coast of Virginia you shall Do your best endeavour to find out a safe fort in the Entrance of some navigable River making Choice of Such a one as runneth furthest into the Land, and if you happen to Discover Divers [diverse] portable [navigable] Rivers and amongst them any one that hath two main branches if the Difference be not Great make Choice of that which bendeth most towards the Northwest for that way shall You soonest find the Other Sea."

Jamestown, as it looked in 1607. The settlement is protected by a ditch and palisade (a high fence made of stakes) . A baking oven is outside the wall (why outside?). In the center is a church. Most of the houses have thatched roofs made from river grass or reeds, but some are covered with tree bark (an idea borrowed from the Indians). Today most of the site lies below the James River. But you can visit a reconstructed Jamestown nearby.

gion had been taken to Spain, baptized a Christian, educated, and returned to his people. That prince had far more schooling than most of the Englishmen who now wished to invade his land. The Englishmen didn't seem to know any of that. They thought of the Indians as savages.

The Englishmen spent a few weeks exploring the bay area. They feasted on strawberries ("four times bigger and better than ours in England"), ate oysters ("which were very large and delicate in taste"), and noticed grapevines ("in bigness as a man's thigh"). The oysters and mussels "lay on the ground as thick as stones; we opened

John Smith's portrait labels him "Admirall of New England." (Today admiral is spelled with one l. Do you see any other old-fashioned spellings?) Even if this wasn't an official title bestowed by the king, Smith deserved it: he not only explored and mapped Virginia but charted the New England coast from Cape Cod to Maine.

26

some, and found in many of them pearls…as for sturgeon [there were so many of these fish] all the world cannot be compared to it."

They planted a cross at Cape Henry, thanked God for their safe voyage, and watched as Captain Newport opened a sealed metal box. The box had been entrusted to him by the London Company. (Newport would soon sail back to England.) He opened the box and read six names and his own. They were to be members of a council and elect a president. One of the names was a surprise. It was John Smith; he was locked up in the ship's belly.

Smith was of yeoman (YO-mun) stock—and feisty; he was not one of the gentlemen. He had angered some of those gentlemen and they had put him in chains. They were planning to send him back to England. Now they would have to work with him.

The instructions in the box said they were to go inland, up a river, and find a suitable place for their colony. So they left the mouth of the Chesapeake Bay and sailed up a river they called the James, to a site they named Jamestown.

Several men, including John Smith and Christopher Newport, went on, up the James River, in search of a passage to China. They had no idea of the size of the country. When they saw breaking waves, they were sure they had found the western coast and the Pacific Ocean. John Smith wrote in his log of the "ocean ahead."

They soon discovered that the waves were caused by water tumbling over rapids in the river. They were at a site that would someday be the city of Richmond. The river would not let them go farther.

All those Jameses—the James River and Jamestown—were named to honor the new king, James I. When Queen Elizabeth died in 1603, still unmarried and childless, her cousin James was brought from Scotland to become king of the United Kingdom of Scotland and England.

King James had worked out a kind of deal with the Spaniards. It went like this: we English will stop raiding your ships if you Spaniards will promise not to attack our settlers. So the new settlers weren't as worried about Spanish attackers as they might have been in the 16th century. As it turned out, there may have been Spanish spies among them.

But it was gold that was on their mind when they reached Jamestown, and they soon began searching for it. They also built rough huts for shelter and a triangular fort for protection.

Jamestown was almost an island, with a narrow sandbar link to the mainland. It would be easy to defend against Indian raids or against ships, just in case the Spaniards did decide to come up the river. Besides, deep water touched the land. They could sail right up to the site and tie their ships to trees.

A *yeoman* was a small farmer who cultivated his own land (it was the area of land that was small, not necessarily the farmer). John Smith came from a yeoman background—he himself did other things with his life.

James I wasn't a bad man. He was very learned about many subjects, but couldn't deal with people very well. He was kind and generous to his friends, but tactless with those he didn't know. He disapproved of tobacco smoking because he thought it filthy and disgusting, but he never washed himself—and he had terrible table manners.

27

From The Proceedings of the English Colony in Virginia, 1612: "There was no talk, no hope, no work, but dig gold, wash gold, refine gold, load gold, such a bruit [noise] of gold, as one mad fellow desired to be buried in the sands, lest they should by their art make gold of his bones."

As it turned out, they couldn't have picked a worse spot. The land was swampy, the drinking water was bad; it was hot in summer and bone-chilling in winter. The mosquitoes drove the settlers crazy and carried malaria germs.

They might have handled all that if they had been a decent bunch. But, for the most part, they were lazy and vain and fought among themselves. And their first two leaders were incompetent—which means they made a mess of the job.

All were men; they brought no women. Remember, most were gentlemen, with no training or taste for hard work. To be fair, they had been misled about the New World. They expected to find gold at their feet, and they wasted valuable time looking for it. And there wasn't a farmer among them.

To make things worse, the London Company, which had paid for the voyage, showed poor sense. It gave all the colonists salaries and did not allow them to own property. No one had a reason to work hard, because the hard workers got the same pay as those who did nothing.

Besides all that, they had bad luck—lots of bad luck. The worst may have been that they brought some English germs across the sea. One was a typhoid fever germ that killed many of them. Tidewater Virginia had other germs (especially dysentery germs) that made some sicken and die. The Indians killed still others. Some starved. What happened to those eager men and boys who had stood on London's docks in December? Fewer than half of them saw another December.

Yet the news wasn't all bad. This was the first English colony that survived in the New World. A few things had to go right to make that happen. One man, more than any other, helped make things go right. He was short, scrappy, red-bearded John Smith—who had come to Virginia in chains. He was Jamestown's third president and a born leader, even though many of the voyagers didn't like him.

The settlers built small houses of wattle and daub—sticks and clay. They finished just in time to stave off their first Indian attack on May 26, 1607.

5 John Smith

Smith's Turk's head coat of arms. The Latin motto means "Vanquish and live."

The Jamestown colony might not have survived without Captain John Smith. He was a tough, no-nonsense man who worked hard and expected everyone else to do the same. Some people admired him; others hated him.

Pocahontas admired him and saved his life—twice. She was a bright-eyed Indian princess who was about 12 years old when the settlers first came to Virginia. The pale-skinned men and their strange ways intrigued her and she came to visit them often. Sometimes she just turned cartwheels in the middle of the Jamestown settlement; sometimes she brought food. It was John Smith who seemed to interest her most. In him she recognized a person whose intelligence and curiosity matched her own. Like her father, the great Powhatan, Smith seemed fearless.

Many of the settlers hated Smith, but they recognized that he was a leader. When he went back to England, even his enemies missed him. They said he was a braggart and that he couldn't possibly have done all the things he said he had done. He might have exaggerated a bit, but he really did do those things—like selling his schoolbooks and running away to sea. Or going off to Hungary to fight the Turks. There, on one bloody afternoon, Smith beheaded three Turks. A grateful Hungarian prince granted him a coat of arms with three Turks' heads emblazoned on it.

He wasn't a Hungarian hero for long; he was captured and sent as a slave to Constantinople, where a Turkish woman bought him. But her relatives didn't think much of him, and he was sold again. This time he killed his master, escaped, got thrown into the Mediterranean Sea, wandered through Russia, Poland, and Germany doing heroic things, and ended up in North Africa fighting pirates.

That first summer in Jamestown the settlers barely made it. "Our drink was water, our lodging, castles in the air," they reported. "With this lodging and diet, our extreme toil in bearing and planting palisades strained and bruised us....From May to September those that escaped lived upon sturgeon and sea crabs. Fifty in this time were buried."

Naturally someone who liked adventure the way John Smith did would be attracted to the adventure of a new world. Besides, like Sir Walter Raleigh, he had an idea that America could someday be an English land. He understood that there was more to be gained in the New World than gold. He realized that there were great opportunities for men and women with energy and courage.

John Smith was 28 when he took over the leadership of the Jamestown colony, and things were in a bad way. This was his motto: "If any would not work, neither should he eat." There were some grumblers, but everyone wanted to eat. So everyone worked.

Smith went and got food from the Indians. He learned their language and he learned the ways they hunted and fished. He had been a soldier and he was tough, but he was also fair and honest; the Powhatans soon understood that. They respected him and he respected them. They called him "werowance," or chief, of Jamestown. And that was what he was.

The Native Americans seemed undecided about how to act toward these strangers on their land. What would you have done if you were a Powhatan? How would you have treated the English leader, John Smith?

He had goods they wanted—axes and shovels and blankets—so they traded with him. He was a natural trader. He took his English goods to their villages and he came back to Jamestown with boatloads of corn. They told him of the prediction: that men from the east would destroy their villages. He told them he came in peace. Still, the Indians couldn't seem to make up their minds.

Sometimes they entertained Smith with dances and feasting. Other times they tried to kill him. Once he was brought before an Indian werowance and he expected to die. He pulled out his compass, showed how it worked, talked about the heavens and the earth, and soon had a tribe of friends. Another time he was taken to the great Powhatan, who seemed to have several Indian warriors ready to beat his brains out. But Pocahontas, who was the Powhatan's favorite daughter, came to his rescue. She

Those early days weren't all misery. After their first Christmas in Virginia, Captain Smith wrote, "We were never more merry, nor fed more plenty of good oysters, fish, flesh, wild fowl and good bread, nor never had better fires in England than in the dry smoky houses of Kecoughtan."

In a page from John Smith's *Generall Historie of Virginia*, Smith lies captive before the Powhatan while Pocahontas pleads for his life to be spared.

King Powhatan comands C: Smith to be flaine, his daughter Pokahontas beggs his life his thankfullnes and how he fubiected 39 of their kings, reads ye history

This engraving is a copy of a 1587 map of "Virginia" by John White that influenced mapmakers for decades. The area shown is now part of the Carolinas. At the mouth of the big river in the middle is Roanoke ("Roainac") Island.

Rough Justice

In some parts of our country, when a criminal is found guilty of a serious crime, such as murder, he can be sentenced to death by the judge. A death sentence is called capital punishment. How did capital punishment start in this country? The English brought the tradition with them. (Some Indian tribes practiced capital punishment, too.)

It didn't take long for the settlers to use capital punishment—a few months. The first execution was in the Jamestown colony in 1607. The victim was not a common criminal, but a member of a prominent English family and one of the seven-man ruling council of the Jamestown colony. His name was Captain George Kendall. His crime was treason. The colonists believed Kendall was a spy for the Spanish. Kendall tried to escape aboard the ship *Discovery,* but was captured and condemned to die. He was executed by a firing squad.

put her head on Smith's, and Powhatan let him live. Was it a pre-arranged ceremony, or did Pocahontas actually save his life? No one knows for sure, but the Indians ended up adopting Smith into their tribe and making him an honorary chief. Now he was a member of Pocahontas's family.

When some other Indians tried to ambush Smith, Pocahontas warned him of the trap. Cats are supposed to have nine lives. John Smith had even more. While exploring the Chesapeake Bay, he was stung by a deadly stingray and was in such agony that he had his grave dug. He recovered—and ate the stingray. (The place where this happened, near the mouth of the Rappahannock River in Virginia, is now called Stingray Point.)

John Smith was asleep in his boat when some gunpowder exploded. It "tore the flesh from his body and thighs nine to ten inches square....To quench the tormenting fire, frying him in his clothes, he leaped over board in the deep river, where...he was near drowned." Smith was so badly wounded that he had to return to England. Pocahontas was told he was dead.

John Smith never got back to Virginia. But he did get to New England, which he named, and he mapped its coast as he had mapped much of Virginia. He wrote many books and became famous because of them. "I am no compiler by hearsay, but have been a real actor," he said. And so he was. We still read his books today, because they are so interesting.

6 The Starving Time

It didn't matter how many pigs there were if you couldn't get out to kill them.

The Laydons named their baby *Virginia*.

Before John Smith left for England, he counted the food in the storehouses at Jamestown. "Ten weeks' provisions in the stores," he wrote. It was October of 1609. Was there enough food to get through the winter? Smith seemed to think so. He expected the Indians to supply corn, as they had before. Besides, the settlers had hens, chickens, and goats—and so many pigs that a nearby island was called Hog Island. In addition to all that, the woods abounded with deer, rabbit, and squirrel; the river was thick with fish, frogs, and oysters.

There were new people in Jamestown, brought from England by Captain Newport. Two were women: Mrs. Thomas Forrest, the wife of a settler, and her maid, Anne Burras. Anne Burras's arrival led to a happy event, which a poet, Stephen Vincent Benét, imagined three and a half centuries later:

> —And the first white wedding held on Virginia ground
> Will marry no courtly dame to a cavalier
> But Anne Burras, lady's maid, to John Laydon, laborer,
> After some six weeks' courtship—a Fall wedding
> When the leaves were turning and the wild air sweet,
> And we know no more than that but it sticks in the mind,
> For they were serving-maid and laboring man
> And yet, while they lived (and they had not long to live),
> They were half of the first families in Virginia.

The Laydons soon had a baby. Can you guess what they named her?

Still more colonists arrived. Now there were many mouths to feed, but most people were optimistic. Everyone thought Jamestown had seen the worst of its troubles.

Everyone was wrong. That winter of 1609–1610 was as awful a time as any in American history. It was called the Starving Time.

Captain George Percy, who was now governor of the Jamestown colony, said the settlers felt the "sharp prick of hunger which no man can truly describe but he who hath tasted the bitterness thereof."

They ate "dogs, cats, rats and mice," said Percy, as well as "serpents and snakes" and even boots and shoes.

> There were never Englishmen left in a foreign country in such misery....Our food was but a small can of barley, sod in water, to five men a day...our men night and day groaning in every corner of the fort most pitiful to hear...some departing out of the world, many times three or four in a night; in the morning their bodies trailed out of their cabins like dogs to be buried.

What happened? Some historians say the Starving Time was an Indian war against the English invaders. The Powhatan may have decided to get rid of the settlers by starving them. He wouldn't trade with them. He laid siege to Jamestown. That means armed Indians wouldn't let anyone in or out. The settlers couldn't hunt or fish. They could hardly get to their chickens and pigs. The gentlemen ate the animals that were inside the stockade—without much sharing. That made the others angry. Soon there was nothing for anyone to eat.

A few escaped. "Many of our men this Starving Time did run away unto the savages, whom we never heard of after," Percy wrote.

In London the Spanish ambassador learned of the misery in Virginia. (Some said there was a Spanish spy at Jamestown, but a spy wasn't needed; the disaster was common news in London.) The ambassador urged the Spanish king to send a ship and finish off the English colony. The Spaniards could have done it easily. So could the Indians, who never went that far. (What do you think American history might have been like if either of those things had happened?)

Finally, in May 1610, two English ships tied up at Jamestown's docks. Of the 500 people who were in Jamestown in October, when John Smith left for London, only 60 were still alive.

Would Powhatan have behaved differently if John Smith had been around? This is one of those historical questions that are interesting to think about.

When the new governor, Sir Thomas Gates, arrived in Jamestown after the terrible winter, it looked to him "rather as the ruins of some ancient fortification than that any people living might now inhabit it."

The Indians had power, the settlers were starved (although they look well-fed in this picture). One man was so hungry he seems to have eaten his dead wife.

7 A Lord, A Hurricane, A Wedding

Shakespeare wrote a play, *The Tempest*, after reading about the storm that wrecked the *Sea Venture* off Bermuda.

A *flotilla* is a group or small fleet of ships. *Unholsome* is the old spelling. Today we would write it as *unwholesome*. (See opposite page.)

On board ship the expression *all hands* means "all people."

The people who walked off the two English ships in May of 1610 were horrified by what they saw. Jamestown was a wreck. Fear of Indians had kept everyone inside the fort through the cold winter. The settlers had been forced to burn their buildings to keep warm. By spring there were hardly any buildings left. The few survivors looked like skeletons. "We are starving!" they gasped.

Those on the ships had been through an ordeal themselves. On their way to Jamestown yellow fever broke out. There was no treatment for the disease then, so people died and their bodies had to be thrown overboard. They were barely over the epidemic when they ran into a fierce Atlantic hurricane.

Do you know what a hurricane at sea is like? Here it is: phenomenal, roaring winds; towering, crashing waves; fierce, crackling lightning; ear-splitting thunder. One ship, the *Catch,* went down; all hands lost. The *Sea Venture,* with sturdy Christopher Newport as captain, was wrecked on coral rocks. Luckily the rocks were within wading distance of the island of Bermuda. If you have to be shipwrecked, Bermuda is not a bad place to be. The voyagers set to work and built two new ships, the *Patience* and the *Deliverance.* They were eager to get to Jamestown and start a new life there. They imagined that the colony was thriving.

You know what they found at Jamestown. Are you surprised that they decided to leave? They had had enough of this New World. On June 7, 1610, everyone marched out of the wretched settlement, climbed aboard ship, said, "Goodbye, Jamestown," and headed for England.

They didn't get far. Lord de la Warr (what state is named for him?) was on his way up the James River with a big flotilla and 300 settlers. He was the new governor, and a good one. He made them turn around and start Jamestown again.

Lord de la Warr called Jamestown "a very…unholsome place." Still, he stayed. The colonists set to work. They cleaned, fixed, and built. The Indians continued to make their lives miserable, but now the settlers fought back. Then a few Indians and a few colonists began to trade. Some Englishmen began going up the rivers to trade with distant tribes. Tom Savage, who had lived as an adopted son of the Powhatan, was able to interpret for both peoples.

More ships came. Artisans and laborers arrived, together with "gentlemen of quality" and more livestock.

And still many died, not from starvation but from the diseases that abounded in the damp atmosphere at Jamestown.

Ætatis suæ 21. Aᵒ. 1616.

Matoaks als Rebecka daughter to the mighty Prince Powhatan Emperour of Attanoughkomouck als Virginia converted and baptized in the Christian faith, and Wife to the worᵖˡ Mʳ Tho: Rolff.

Lord de la Warr was one of those who got sick. He went back to England, and Sir Thomas Dale took command. Dale understood the need for a healthier settlement. So one was built at a great bend of the James River, near the falls that John Smith had mistaken for the Pacific Ocean. The new settlement was named Henrico, for Henry, the king's oldest son. It had "two fair rows of houses," three "store houses," a hospital, and a "fair and handsome church." All of it was constructed in four months— Thomas Dale saw to that. Dale was a stern man, strict and religious. Anyone who swore, broke a rule, or didn't work got whipped. Three offenses and you were executed. You can see why everyone worked.

Henrico soon had a visitor. Unfortunately she was dragged there. Her name was Pocahontas.

The Indian princess was visiting some Potomac Indians when an Englishman, on a trading expedition, lured her onto his ship and wouldn't let her off. He took Pocahontas as a hostage to Henrico,

Pocahontas had two names. Her real name was Matoax. It means "little snow feather." Pocahontas, her nickname, means "playful." Then Pocahontas married John Rolfe. She was baptized and given a third name: Rebecca.

What is a hostage? Where do we hear the word today?

English noblemen like Lord
de la Warr *(above)* often have
two names: a title (such as
Lord de la Warr) and their
own given and family names.
Lord de la Warr's name was
Thomas West.

held her there, taught her the Christian religion, and gave her a new name, Rebecca.

Now it happened that a young Englishman named John Rolfe had a plantation nearby. He fell in love with the beautiful Indian princess and she fell in love with him.

Rolfe wrote to Governor Dale, asking to marry Pocahontas "to whom my heart and best thoughts are, and have a long time been so entangled, and enthralled in so intricate a labyrinth, that I was even wearied to unwind myself thereout."

It was a fine wedding, and it took place in the church at Jamestown. The Powhatan wouldn't come. Perhaps he feared a trap, or perhaps he was sad to see his daughter leave the Indian world. He sent two of her brothers and her uncle, Chief Opechancanough. They came wearing handsome garments of leather, furs, feathers, and beads. Pocahontas's marriage helped bring peace between Indians and colonists.

Soon Pocahontas had a baby and John Rolfe was so proud he took his family to England. There Pocahontas charmed everyone—even King James. (And King James didn't charm easily; he was a bit of a grouch.) The English people called her Lady Rebecca and treated her as the princess that she was. People fussed over her and pointed to her when she walked down the street. She was a celebrity. But she must have longed for a familiar face, someone she could talk to in her native language. And then she learned that John Smith was alive! She expected him to come and see her at once, but he didn't. She waited and waited. Finally, when he did come, she was so hurt that at first she wouldn't even talk to him.

John Smith had been honored by her father. He was a member of her family. How could he ignore her? But Smith seemed different, and awkward. Perhaps he didn't know how to be her brother now that she wore a long dress like a proper Englishwoman. Perhaps Pocahontas herself didn't know in which world she belonged. When John Rolfe decided to go back to Virginia, she didn't want to go. She didn't feel at all well when they boarded a ship and sailed down the Thames River. Before they reached the open sea, she was so sick that her husband took her off the ship. It was smallpox. Pocahontas died, and was buried in the churchyard at Gravesend, a town that is now part of London, but in those days was in the country. She was 22.

Let's take ourselves back in time to Jamestown. The Powhatan has not yet learned that his beloved daughter is dead. When he does, the peace will be finished. The Indians will attack. They will kill settlers, burn their homes, and try to drive them from the land. But now, for a while, there is calm.

8 A Share in America

Indian corn and an "Indian" jaybird illustrated a booklet advertising the New World's attractions.

More English ships sail for Jamestown…and more settlers…and more again. An English poet writes:

> God will not let us fail.
> Let England know our willingness,
> For that our work is good;
> We hope to plant a nation
> Where none before hath stood.

English men and women begin to spread out beyond Jamestown. They are settling in the New World.

It seems as if everyone in England wants to be part of the American adventure. And everyone can be part of it by giving money to the Virginia Company—the new name of the London Company—the outfit that is paying for all the exploration. The Virginia Company is a stock company, just like stock companies today. You can buy shares in the company; your money helps pay the company's expenses; if there are profits you will get your share of them.

Lords, knights, gentlemen, merchants, and plain citizens buy shares in the Virginia Company. The Archbishop of Canterbury, the Earl of Pembroke, famous Londoners, and unknown squires—all are among the investors.

The Spanish ambassador in London writes to King Philip that "fourteen earls and barons have given 40,000 ducats, the merchants give much more, and there is no poor little man nor woman who is not willing to subscribe something… much as I have written to your Majesty of the determina-

How long would you last in this armor—on a humid summer's day in Virginia, out looking for deer?

37

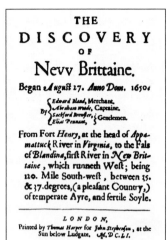

THE
DISCOVERY
OF
Nevv Brittaine.

Began *August* 27. *Anno Dom.* 1650;

By {
Edward Bland, Merchant.
Abraham wood, Captaine.
Sackford Brewster,
Elias Pennant,
} Gentlemen.

From Fort *Henry*, at the head of *Appa-
mattuck* River in *Virginia*, to the Fals
of *Blandina*, first River in *New Brittaine*, which runneth Weſt; being
120. Mile South-weſt, between 35.
& 37. degrees, (a pleaſant Country,)
of temperate Ayre, and fertile Soyle.

LONDON,
Printed by *Thomas Harper* for *John Stephenson*, at the
Sun below Ludgate. *M.DC.LI.*

The early promoters of the Virginia settlements had an uphill job, for everyone in England had heard of the terrible experiences of the first Jamestown colonists.

Class System

To some extent, the English will succeed in bringing their class society to Virginia. An upper class of landowning aristocrats will be the leaders. There will be a middle class of yeomen owning small farms. The lower class will be made up of indentured servants and slaves. The Virginia aristocracy will differ from the English aristocracy in an important way: the idea that gentlemen should not work will be rejected in the New World.

tion they have formed here to go to Virginia, it seems to me that I still fall short of the reality."

Some of those people expect to make money from the gold that they are sure will be found. Many just want to take part in a great national venture. Some want to save the North American Indians from the Spaniards. In England people have read stories about the way some Spaniards treat the Indians: how they make them dig gold, how they starve them, how they make slaves of them. Good people are horrified.

They don't realize that English men and women are just like Spanish men and women. Some are good, some are not so good.

Some of the not-so-goods come to Jamestown. It is understandable that they would. Some people leave England because they are brave and curious; some are looking for riches or a better life. But others come because they are criminals and unwanted in England.

An Englishman named William Tucker arranges a powwow with the Pamunkey Indians. He tells them he wants to sign a peace treaty. The Indians give him corn and sign the treaty. Then Tucker suggests they all celebrate by drinking wine. He doesn't tell them he has poisoned the wine: 200 Indians die.

Other Englishmen attack and burn Indian villages, sometimes for no apparent reason, sometimes to revenge the Starving Time.

Meanwhile, back in England, some people are writing of Virginia as a place where Native Americans and Europeans can live side by side and learn about the best of each other's culture. They talk of In-

A 17th-century musketeer demonstrates the workings of his firearm.

dians going to English schools and Englishmen being trained in Indian ways. An English school for the Indians is started at Henrico.

The people who have these fine ideas aren't concerned with gold. They picture an ideal nation where people live happily tending gardens and working at jobs like blowing glass, forging iron, and making perfume.

But the people with the good ideas stay in England. They are making plans for others, and that usually doesn't work. Those who come to Virginia aren't interested in ideal societies. Most have come for adventure, or to get rich, or to get away from their problems in Europe. After they get here, they find it a lot of trouble just trying to stay alive.

Of the first 10,000 settlers who land in Virginia, only 2,000 survive. (What percentage is that?) They die of disease, Indian attack, and hunger.

Hunger? In a land of plenty? Yes, even in a land of plenty you need to know how to hunt, or fish, or raise crops, or gather food. You need to adapt yourself to new conditions. If ever you go to a strange land, try and see how the natives live. You will learn a lot. That is what John Smith did. Some of the gentlemen do not learn. They try to be Englishmen in a wilderness.

Picture Jamestown in August. If there were a thermometer it would register 98°F. The English gentlemen sometimes wear 60-pound suits of metal armor. That makes them feel safe from Indian arrows. Under the armor they wear wool clothing, because that is what they have always worn in England. Now, imagine chopping down a tree in that outfit: your hands are blistered—you've never held an ax before—and the biting flies are driving you crazy. Are you beginning to get angry? Look at the swampy ground. It's full of snakes and frogs and bugs—not the gold you were promised.

So you throw down your ax and decide to go hunting. Maybe you can kill a deer—you've seen plenty of animals. But that heavy musket is a problem. It makes a loud noise when it goes off, and you can't seem to hit anything with it, certainly not anything moving. A musket isn't accurate, like a rifle—but rifles haven't been invented yet. (A musket isn't as accurate as a bow and arrow, either.)

There is another problem I haven't mentioned. You stink. You haven't had a bath—ever. (Well, if you were daring, you may have had one last year.) Baths are considered unhealthy. Now remember, it is August and you are wearing all those clothes. Phew! If the deer aren't scared off by your loud, clanking armor, the smell will soon have them running. Indian hunters are quiet as falling leaves. They take off most of their clothes in summer; they bathe in the river. It is no wonder the Indians think the Englishmen are savages.

Tidewater Virginia's diseases are new to the Europeans and kill many of them. But the Virginia diseases are not as deadly to the newcomers as the European diseases are to the Native Americans. Tribes are being wiped out.

Wait a few chapters and you'll see: there were fewer deaths in New England. The colder climate seemed to keep some germs under control, and the community there was better organized.

9 Jamestown Makes It

Taino Indians of the Bahamas grew tobacco; Spaniards copied its Taino name, *tabaco.*

European tobacco merchants advertised their product with fanciful pictures of the exotic New World and its inhabitants.

At last the settlers found gold. Gold in the form of a leaf. A leaf that dried to a golden brown and could be put in a pipe and smoked. That tobacco leaf made people rich; it made the Virginia colony prosperous.

King James hated tobacco. He thought it unhealthy and he was right. But there is a limit to what even kings can do when money is involved. Growing tobacco was very profitable, especially after John Rolfe, Pocahontas's husband, developed a sweet variety that was all the rage in England.

But there was a problem. It takes hard fieldwork to grow tobacco, and Englishmen were not anxious to work in the fields. Besides that, even the best farmers could tend only a limited number of tobacco plants. So if you wanted to get rich by growing tobacco, you had to have people working for you. The more people you had, the more tobacco you could grow. The more tobacco you sold, the richer you would get. That made servants and other workers very valuable in Virginia.

So the Virginians did everything they could think of to get people to come to America. But since most of the settlers were dying, it wasn't easy. Most of those who came were poor or in trouble with the law.

The colonists were so eager to have workers that they were willing to pay for them. Sometimes they paid so much money that ship's captains would kidnap people from the streets of London.

Many of those who came to Virginia started out as indentured servants, and usually they were very poor. Some of them were criminals who were let out of jail if they would agree to come to the colony. You can understand that most people didn't want to go to a land where so many people were dying. The indentured servants didn't have enough money to pay their boat fare to the New World. They had to work for the person who paid the fare. They worked from four to seven years before they were free. That was their time of indenture. Some indentured servants were treated just like slaves.

What about slaves? Were there slaves in Jamestown? Yes, there were. Slavery in the English colonies began without much thought, which is the way bad things often begin.

In 1619 a Dutch ship brought a boatload of Africans to Jamestown. These people had been kidnapped from their homes by African traders and sold to the ship's captain. He in turn sold them to the Virginia settlers. Those first African Virginians were treated like indentured servants. After a few years of working for someone else, they became free. Soon there were Africans who had land of their own—and servants, too. But some colonists got the idea of making black people into slaves. That way they wouldn't have to keep buying workers on the docks. It must have seemed a good idea to people who were desperate for workers. Tobacco agriculture demanded much labor as well as a lot of land. There was an abundance of land in America, but few people willing to do hard work in the fields.

When Indians were enslaved, they ran away. It was difficult for the blacks to run away. Where would they go? Everything was new and strange to them. Gradually laws were passed to trap black people in slavery. It was the beginning of a way of life that would bring misery to many, many innocent African-Americans.

Why did Europeans go to the trouble of importing African slaves instead of forcing Native Americans to work for them? Because the Indians didn't make good slaves. They got sick from Old World diseases, and often they just ran away.

How Tobacco Beat Out Silk

The silkworm is the caterpillar stage of the silk moth. The material the silkworms spin into their cocoons is what makes the silk thread.

King James wanted to start a silk industry in Virginia, and the colonists needed a doctor. Dr. Lawrence Bohune was the perfect man for both tasks: he was a physician and he had scientific curiosity. He planned to experiment with silkworms and also to investigate the native herbs and plants the Indians used for healing purposes. Bohune had visited the colony in 1610 as Lord de la Warr's personal doctor, and he had impressed everyone with his good sense. So when he made plans to bring silkworms to Virginia, the king and the settlers were pleased.

In 1620, Dr. Bohune set sail for Jamestown on a ship named the *Margaret and John*. (It was the very year the Pilgrims arrived in Massachusetts Bay.) After 11 tough weeks at sea, the small ship reached the West Indies and found itself facing two armed Spanish warships. The Spaniards fired their cannons. The English ship was outclassed, a cannonball struck the good doctor, and he fell into the arms of the captain. "Oh, Dr. Bohune, what a disaster this is!" said the captain. With his last breath the doctor replied, "Fight it out, brave man, the cause is good, and the Lord receive my soul."

When the damaged ship limped into Jamestown, the doctor was dead and the silkworms had all been lost at sea. King James had hoped that silk would replace tobacco as Virginia's gold. It never did.

10 1619— A Big Year

If the colony was to survive, it had to grow. That meant sending women as well as men.

The English found those first years in America really hard. Remember, four out of five of the first 10,000 settlers died soon after they arrived in Virginia. Most people would have given up—but not the English. The harder the challenge, the more determined they became.

The year 1619 was a turning point. After 1619 you could tell the English were in America to stay. It was a year of many firsts in Virginia:

- first boatload of Africans
- first boatload of women
- first labor strike
- first time English settlers are allowed to own land
- first elected lawmakers.

That is a lot for any year. You already know about that boatload of Africans. Now, about those women. They, too, were sold on the docks.

"Do you want a wife?"

"It will cost you 120 pounds of tobacco."

Those are the terms when a shipload of women arrives in Jamestown in 1619. These are poor women who are unable to pay the cost of their Atlantic journey. They want a new life in this new land. The lonely men want wives. There will be instant romances on the docks. What do you think of these women? Do you think they are scared? Courageous? Crazy?

A few white women have already been to Jamestown, but sending an entire boatload of them to be wives means that the English plan to stay and make homes in America. The French, who are settling in the North, are less likely to send women. Still, in 1619, the men in Jamestown outnumber the women by eight to one.

Some historians think the reason there was much violence in Jamestown was because many more men than women and children lived there. Do you think that is true? Do you think men living alone fight more than people in families? That is something to discuss.

In 1619 the Virginia Company lets the settlers have land of their own. That gives them a reason to work hard.

The first workers' strike in British America happens in 1619. Polish workers at Jamestown, who are glassmakers, demand the same rights as Englishmen. They get those rights and go back to work. There are Poles, Dutch, Germans, and Italians at Jamestown. Do you think it strange that they all want English rights? What about their own rights?

The answer to that is very simple. English men and women have more rights and freedom than people do in other European nations. They expect those same rights in America and so do people from other nations who come to the English colonies.

John Smith said no one would come to the New World "to have less freedom." The Charter of the Virginia Company said, "all and every of the persons...which shall dwell and inhabit within every or any of the said several colonies and plantations, and every of their children...shall have and enjoy all liberties...as if they had been abiding and born, within this our realm of England." That means that nobody will lose freedom if he moves from England to America.

In 1619, a group of lawmakers—known as "burgesses"—is elected to make laws. They form an assembly called the House of Burgesses. In England laws are made by Parliament. The House of Burgesses gives the Virginians their own form of Parliament. That has never happened in a colony before.

By the way, do you know what a colony is?

A colony is land controlled by a distant, or foreign, nation. In the 17th century many European nations have colonies in America as well as in other parts of the world. Those colonies are not all alike. In the Spanish colonies no Europeans except Spaniards are allowed to settle. France admits only Catholics. The English colonies have open doors.

Think about that for a minute. That decision, way back in the 1600s, to let all kinds of people settle in the English colonies, made a big difference to our country. We would become a pluralistic society. (What does that mean?)

After seven years' work, those who wanted were given their own land. Captain Smith said, "When our people were fed out of the common store, and laboured jointly together, glad was he who could slip from his labour, or slumber over his tasks, he cared not how; nay, the most honest among them would hardly take so much true paines in a week, as now for themselves they will do in a day."

A *realm* is the kingdom or country where a ruler holds sway.

Abiding means permanent or lasting.

43

A Hostage Swap

In 1611, Captain John Clark was a pilot on one of three ships bound for Virginia. (Like an airplane pilot, a ship's pilot is expected to guide his craft safely.) Clark and his ships (Christopher Newport was in charge of the expedition) made it to Virginia. They hadn't been there long when a Spanish ship sailed into Chesapeake Bay. A Spanish officer came ashore and was taken hostage. To get even, the Spaniards captured Clark and sailed off to Spain. Five years later the two prisoners were exchanged in London. In 1620, the Virginia Company asked John Clark to pilot a ship to Virginia. It was the *Mayflower,* and it didn't quite reach its destination.

The Virginia Company was so eager to get women to come to America that it sometimes resorted to buying girls from their families or even kidnapping them from their homes.

Now that you know about colonies, let's get back to the House of Burgesses. In the 17th century, laws for colonies were made in the home country, or by appointed governors and their councils. The House of Burgesses changed that.

England was letting colonists make laws for themselves. That was a big first in history. (An English governor did have *veto power* over the burgesses. What is a veto? Okay, you can do some work. Go to the dictionary and look that word up. The governor didn't use the veto very often.)

This is something you should remember: the House of Burgesses, formed in 1619, gave America its first representative government. It was the beginning of self-government in America.

Whoops! Hold on, that isn't quite true. Some Indian tribes had representative government. The House of Burgesses was the first representative assembly in the European colonies.

It was only a dozen years since those three small ships were tied to the trees at Jamestown and the English colonists were doing something very unusual. They were making laws for themselves.

11 Indians vs. Colonists

If the European settlements were to grow, they had to have the Indians' land. And the Indians weren't about to give it up easily.

The Powhatan Indians played football with a small ball and a goal. The men played one set of rules, the women and children another. But for all the players, speed and dexterity were important. The Indians also enjoyed a game called "chunkey," which was played with a disk-shaped stone and slim poles eight or ten feet long. The idea was to roll the disk as far as possible and then throw the pole and try to hit it— or knock your opponent's pole away from its target disk.

From the time of Columbus the pattern was the same. The newcomers and the Indians would meet as friends and trade with each other. Then something would happen. Often an Indian was killed or sold into slavery, and the Indians would strike back. Sometimes they showed remarkable patience. Sometimes they were just waiting for the right moment. For the Native Americans were much like the New Americans: good and bad, fierce and gentle. Warriors on both sides went too far. The massacres were horrible.

At first the Indian leaders tried to live in peace with the settlers. But some of them realized that it would not work, that it would be the end of Indian ways. The Europeans used up land. They cut the forests and filled the land with people. Indians were hunters. To keep their way of life, the woods had to be protected. Wild animals need woods to live in, and hunters need wild animals.

Most Europeans understood that, too. One Virginia governor said, "Either we must clear the Indians out of the country, or they must clear us out." The members of the House of Burgesses ordered three expeditions to drive out the Indians "in order that they have no chance to harvest their crops or rebuild their wigwams."

There was another problem: arrogance (which means thinking you are better than others). In the 17th century arrogance was often tied to religion.

What do you think about this Native American cartoonist's version of the Pilgrims' Thanksgiving story?

Fields of Blood

Not all white people feared and hated Indians. John Lawson, a traveler in Carolina in 1700, wrote in a book about his journey: "We look upon them with Scorn and Disdain, [yet] ...for all our Religion and Education, we possess more Moral Deformities and Evils than these savages do....We make way for a Christian Colony through a Field of Blood, and defraud, and make away with those that one day may be wanted in this world." *John Lawson founded a new settlement himself. He was later captured and killed by Tuscarora Indians.*

This engraving, called *William Penn's Treaty with the Indians,* is based on a famous picture painted by Benjamin West in 1771. Edward Hicks borrowed some of West's ideas for his picture of the same event, shown on page 108.) Artists often had engravings made of their most popular works. Engraving was cheap: it allowed ordinary people who couldn't afford oil paintings to have art in their homes, and it allowed artists to reach a wider public. Why do you think this image—of whites and Indians at peace—was popular enough to be engraved?

Many Christians believed that anyone who was not Christian must be inferior. (The Aztecs believed those who weren't Aztec were inferior.)

Before long, that arrogance would become racism. Some whites believed themselves better than all Indians. Some believed themselves better than all blacks. History shows that racists are troublemakers and often the worst of their own race. There were bigots and racists in early America and they made trouble. Some of them wanted to kill all the Indians. (And some Indians wanted to kill all whites.)

However, the real problem was the fight for control of land. Even when Indians and settlers were friendly, it usually didn't last long. The newcomers wanted Indian land, and naturally the Indians didn't want to give it up. Some fair-minded white leaders respected the Indians and wanted to share the land, but they were never able to control the land-hungry settlers.

In 1737 the Delaware Indian chief Lappawinsoe signed an agreement that gave Pennsylvania colonists all the land they could cover on foot in a day and a half. Instead of walking leisurely, as the Indians expected, the colonists sent runners. Lappawinsoe was shocked and felt the Indians had been swindled.

12 Massacre in Virginia, Poverty in England

Opechancanough was a sachem, an important Indian chief and wise man.

Just when things seemed to be going well for the colonists, Pocahontas's uncle, the sachem Opechancanough, decided to try to get rid of them all. Some historians think that Opechancanough was the Indian prince who had been taken to Spain by Spanish priests, educated, and returned to his people. Whether he was or not, everyone agrees that he was intelligent and crafty, and that he hated the white men who were stealing his land.

In 1622 Opechancanough was an old man. Perhaps he thought it was his last chance to save his people. So he planned a great massacre. Indians knocked on the colonists' doors—pretending to be friendly—and then they murdered and scalped. They might have killed everyone if an Indian boy, Chanco, hadn't warned the men and women at Jamestown. Chanco had been treated kindly by the settlers and had become a Christian. The settlements outside Jamestown didn't get warned. Hundreds of English men, women, and children were killed in the Great Massacre of 1622.

King James was upset; there were too many deaths in Virginia. He set up a government investigation, and then he closed down the Virginia Company. The stockholders were wiped out; their stock was now worthless. King James took Virginia; it became a royal colony. Actually, the king didn't spend much time thinking about the Virginia colony; it was too far away. And he had problems, big problems, at home.

James believed that God had given him the right to rule—he called it "divine right." He thought that divine right meant he could do almost anything he wanted to. Parliament didn't agree, and Parliament controlled

Opechancanough never gave up. In 1644 his warriors attacked Jamestown again. He was so old and feeble he had to be carried about on a bed. Attendants held his eyelids open so he could see. But his mind had not lost its power.

To *massacre* (MASS-uh-ker) means to "kill brutally" and often in large numbers.

After the Jamestown Massacre the English had an excuse for killing Indians, and the bloodshed became intense. Killings were followed by revenge raids, more killings, and more revenge—on both sides.

47

In what languages was the Bible first written? See if you can find the answer.

To **dispute** means to "argue." To **harangue** means to "talk or lecture someone very forcefully." **Drivel** is stupid talk.

Bibles and Books

The King James Bible is made up of two parts: the Old Testament and the New Testament. These books, or parts of them, have other names, too. The Old Testament is also the *Hebrew Bible;* and the first five books (do you know their names?) in the Old Testament make up the Jewish *Torah.* The Greek name for the first five books is the *Pentateuch* (PEN-tuh-tewk). The first four books of the New Testament are the *Gospels.* Another name for the King James Bible is the "Authorized Version"—because its publication was authorized by the king himself.

most of the money in England. Parliament wouldn't give James the cash he wanted. Things got edgy.

James was a thoughtful man who might have made a fine professor. While he was on the throne the Bible was translated into English. That translation is called the "King James Bible." It was read in most Protestant churches in America until the 20th century. Many people think it the most beautiful translation ever.

But what England needed was a strong political leader, not a professor. One historian said King James was "two men—a witty, well-read scholar who wrote, disputed and harangued, and a nervous, drivelling idiot who acted." King Henry IV of France called him "the wisest fool in Christendom." James just wasn't the right type to be a king. He was in the wrong profession.

Let's get into a time capsule and take a look at King James's realm. Things are not going well at all. Farmers, who rent land from the rich landowning lords, are being thrown off their farms. The landlords want the land because of the new craze for sheep raising.

For some reason no one quite understands, the population is growing faster than it has ever done before. Jobs are hard to find. London and the countryside are full of beggars and starving people. Some of them climb on ships and pray for luck and a better life in the New World. Boatloads of people begin crossing the ocean.

Many of those who sail are convicts let out of jail if they will make the voyage. Englishmen write of America as a place to send their poor and troubled.

Some of the settlers are orphans. Many are very young. Heat and germs and Indians will kill most of them, yet they keep coming. Some prosper.

By midcentury (which century?) there are brick houses at Jamestown, a brick church, a fine State House, and plenty of food. For the European settlers, the American Dream has begun. Those who are tough and work hard will find in America a land of opportunity, like no land before it.

Opechancanough and his warriors attacked Jamestown on March 22, 1622. They killed nearly a third of the town's 1,200 inhabitants. It wasn't as one-sided as you might think from the picture. Afterwards, the settlers destroyed many of the Indians' villages, and their crops, too.

America, Land of the Free

From its beginnings, America was a land of freedom and opportunity for all. True or false?

The answer is FALSE.

For many of us, America was a land of humiliation and enslavement.

Africans came to the New World not because they wanted to but because they were taken from their homes by men with powerful weapons. When they protested, they were beaten and killed.

There was big money in it for those who stole them. There was big money in it for those who transported them. There were profits and an easy life for those who bought them.

Slavery was as old as history's records. Probably older. When Moses led the Israelites out of Egypt, they were escaping slavery. The ancient Greeks and Romans kept slaves. But in olden days, slaves were usually the booty of war. If you were captured in battle, you might end up a slave of the enemy. Slavery had nothing to do with skin color. Slaves were sometimes allowed to buy their freedom. Children of slaves were not always enslaved.

It was a Portuguese prince who got the African slave trade started in Europe. Remember Prince Henry the Navigator? In 1442 one of his ships arrived in Portugal with 10 captured Africans. The Portuguese were looking for ways to make money. Africans were good workers. Selling them as slaves would be a profitable business. Prince Henry gave those ten black Africans as a gift to the Roman Catholic Pope. The Pope gave Portugal the right to trade in Africa. But by 1455 the slave trade had become so abusive that Prince Henry tried to stop it. It was too late.

When the New World was discovered, workers were needed to mine its resources and to work its fields. Europeans didn't want those jobs; slaves had no choice.

Slavery in America developed into a terrible and degrading system. To justify that terrible system, a myth arose that blacks were inferior, that they weren't capable people.

Of course, that was just a myth. Africa had produced great cities and beautiful arts. In the 11th century the great African empire of Ghana was flourishing, with "fine houses and solid buildings," and a royal pavilion where pages held gold-tipped swords, horses gleamed in cloths of gold, and princes were "splendidly clad and with gold plaited into their hair." Slaves, in the ancient African kingdoms, were a sign of wealth. It was the way of the world. To be a slave was considered bad luck, not a wrong. The slave trade with other lands thrived—especially with Arabia, Persia, India, even China. Then the Portuguese arrived.

In America an entire way of life depended on the labor of black people. Despite harsh treatment, blacks produced writers, scientists, political leaders, musicians and many others who enriched our nation.

A famous philosopher—named George Santayana—said, "Those who cannot remember the past are condemned to repeat it." What do you think he meant? Do you think he was talking of nations, or people, or both?

One thing he didn't mean was that the same mistakes are made again and again. We will never again allow the kind of slavery we had when this nation began. But there are other forms of slavery. What about drugs? Do they enslave people's minds and bodies? Why do people sell drugs? Why did they have slaves?

In the 20th century slave-labor camps have been the scene of brutality and death for millions of Europeans and Asians. Do you know about them?

Do you know about the system of apartheid (uh-PAR-tide) that existed in South Africa?

American slavery was a horror. We should never pretend it was anything else. But the American system of government lets us correct mistakes. When you study history you see we usually do. Of that we can be proud.

13 The Mayflower: Saints and Strangers

The plaque at St. Peter's Church in Leyden, Holland, put up in memory of the *Mayflower* Pilgrims who once worshiped there.

In December 1620 the *Mayflower* was anchored in Cape Cod harbor. Before the Pilgrims disembarked for good at Plymouth, Mistress Susanna White gave birth on board the ship to the first English baby born in New England, a boy whom she named Peregrine (PAIR-uh-grin). Here is his cradle.

The times were religious—and angry. To understand them we need to review some English history. Remember King Henry VIII? He was the father of Queen Elizabeth. King Henry tossed the Catholic Church out of England long before Jamestown got started. Why Henry did that is an interesting story, but you'll have to look up the details yourself. It had something to do with King Henry's wanting to get married again, and again, and again, and—whew—he had a lot of energy.

The head of the Catholic Church, the Pope, didn't approve of all that marrying. So King Henry founded the Church of England (which is sometimes called the Anglican Church) and made himself its leader.

By the 17th century most English men and women belonged to that church. (As they still do.) It was called the "established church" because it was linked to the government. Since he was king, James was head of the Church of England. The man who actually ran the church was called the Archbishop of Canterbury, and he was appointed by the king.

The Pope lived in Rome in a great palace called the Vatican. That was, and is, the control center for the entire Roman Catholic Church. The Pope is elected by bishops of the Catholic Church.

Except for that matter of control and leadership, the Anglicans and Catholics were much alike, although they didn't think so and often hated and persecuted each other. As I said, the times were

John Smith offered to hire himself out to the Pilgrims as their guide. They told him his book was "better cheap" than he was.

Changing Times

James I brought "new ideas, new goings, new measures, new paces, new heads for your men, for women new faces," according to a poem of the times. It was a time of increasing lawlessness, of new riches for some, of poverty for others. There was growing interest in individual rights; less in community values. People began to focus on material riches rather than religion. All that was confusing and disturbing to many. Have you heard people you know complain about politics and government and the times? The Pilgrims didn't like the politics of their England, so they left.

not only religious, but also intolerant. People took their differences very seriously. Wars were fought over them.

Some Englishmen wanted the differences between Catholics and Protestants to be greater. They felt that King Henry VIII didn't go far enough when he outlawed the Catholic Church. They didn't want the Anglican church service to be at all like the Catholic service. They said they wanted to "purify" the Church of England, so they were called Puritans.

Others wanted to go even further. They believed people could speak directly to God without a priest or bishop at all. They wanted to separate themselves from the Church of England and form congregations of their own. They called themselves "Saints." Other people called them "Separatists." Some people called them troublemakers.

King James would not let the Separatists practice their religion. They had to go to the Church of England or go to jail. Their religion was more important to them than their homes—and sometimes than life itself. Some of the Separatists, especially a group from a village in northeast England called Scrooby, decided to move to Holland, where they were promised religious freedom.

And they got religious freedom in Holland—but they didn't feel at home with the Dutch. They were English, and they liked their own customs and language and villages. When their children started speaking Dutch and forgetting English ways, the people from Scrooby decided it was time to move again. They read John Smith's book, *Description of New England,* and they said, "This time to America."

Anyone who takes a trip for religious purposes is a *pilgrim.* So now these Scrooby people who were called Separatists or Saints had a new name: Pilgrims. They were the first of many, many boatloads of pilgrims who would

The Pilgrims in Holland board ship at Leyden for the first leg of their journey to religious freedom in the New World.

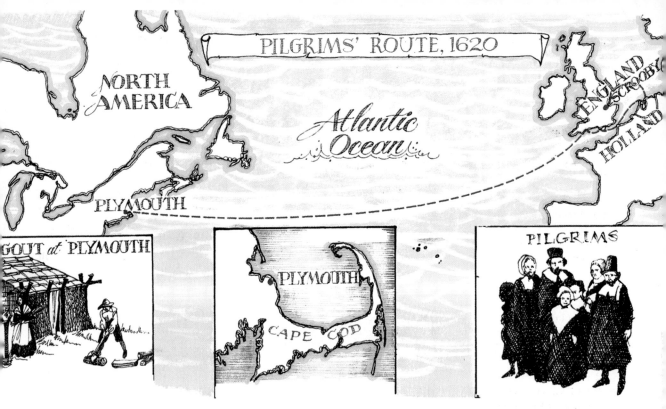

come to America to be free to believe whatever they wanted to believe. They, however, were pilgrims with a capital P: *the* Pilgrims.

The year is 1620. The boat they take is named the *Mayflower*. Of the 102 on board, only about half are Saints; the Scrooby people call the others "Strangers." The Strangers are leaving England for adventure, or because they are unhappy or in trouble. Saints and Strangers have many things in common. Most are from the lower classes; most have a trade; they expect to work hard; they are ambitious; and they can't stand the new ideas that are changing England. All want a better life, but the Saints hope to build a society more perfect than any on earth.

Among the Strangers are 10 indentured servants, a professional soldier, a barrelmaker, four orphans indentured, or "bound," to work without pay until they are 21, and a man soon to be convicted of murder.

Among the Saints is William Bradford, who will be elected as the colony's second governor and will write their story.

It is a terrible voyage, taking 66 days. The ship is small, wet, and foul. The smells are horrid. There is no place to change or wash clothes. Each adult is assigned a space below deck measuring seven by two and a half feet. Children get even less room. None of the passengers is allowed on deck; there is little fresh air below and many are sick. Fresh food soon runs out and then there is hard bread and dried meat that is wet and moldy. But the Pilgrims have onions, lemon juice, and beer to keep them from getting the dreaded scurvy. Amazingly, only one person dies. He is replaced on the roster by a

The word *indentured* originally came from the paper that the contract between master and servant was written on. After they signed it, the paper was torn in half, so that each piece had an *indentation* that fitted into the other piece. The master kept one piece and the servant kept the other. That was the proof of their agreement.

Scurvy is a disease resulting from lack of vitamin C. It makes people bleed easily and causes their teeth to fall out.

The Pilgrims weren't the first Europeans to land at Plymouth Bay. Fishermen, trappers, and explorers, such as the Frenchman Samuel de Champlain, had been there before. Champlain drew this map, showing the Patuxet Indians' villages, in 1605.

Although the *Mayflower* was cramped and uncomfortable, one thing about it was an improvement over many ships. The *Mayflower* had carried wine barrels, and the hold smelled of the wine that had leaked out. Most 17th-century ships stank of garbage.

baby born at sea, Oceanus (oh-shee-ANN-us) Hopkins. Another child, Peregrine White, is born just before they dock.

When they first sight American land, it is at Cape Cod. They planned to go to Virginia, but they are exhausted. Bradford describes Cape Cod as a "hideous and desolate wilderness, full of wild beasts and men." They sail around the cape to a place they see on Smith's map. He has called it Plymouth, after a town in England.

Before they get off the ship, there are matters to attend to. There has been trouble between Saints and Strangers, and it needs to be settled. They must live together peacefully. They need rules and laws and leaders. So they draw up a plan of government, the Mayflower Compact, which establishes a governing body:

> to enact, constitute, and frame such just and equal laws, ordinances, acts, constitutions, offices...for the general good of the Colony; unto which, we promise all due submission and obedience.

That Mayflower Compact is one of the great documents of American history. Here is a group of settlers able to govern themselves; reasonable people who agree to live together under a government of laws. The king doesn't realize what is in the future. This breed of people will not allow others to rule them for long.

Then, wrote Bradford, "being thus arrived in a good harbor, and brought safe to land, they fell upon their knees and blessed the God of Heaven who had brought them over the vast and furious ocean."

When they land, they find empty fields cleared for planting. They will learn that smallpox, caught from white fishermen, has wiped out many of New England's Indians. The Pilgrims believe that God has made the land theirs for the taking.

But it is December—too late to plant crops. Many will hunger and die before spring comes. Fewer than half of the 102 who land will survive the first winter. But no one wants to return to England. These are sturdy folk who intend to start a nation. William Bradford writes of the colony "as one small candle may light a thousand, so the light here kindled hath shone unto many, yea in some sort to our whole nation."

14 Pilgrims, Indians, and Puritans

One way of cooking a turkey on an open fire was in a roasting pan with a tight lid: "For turkey braised, the Lord be praised."

Squanto's real name is Tisquantum. These Native Americans are Algonquians of the Wampanoag tribe, who live in what is now Rhode Island. *Wampanoag* means "eastern people." They hunt, fish, dig for clams, and gather berries and nuts. They are good cooks; they make venison (deer) steak, fish chowders, succotash, cornbread, and maple sugar.

Like the Jamestown colonists, the Pilgrims have picked a poor site. The New England coast is cold and wind-whipped; the land is rocky, the soil is thin. But these industrious people will use the sea and the forest to sustain themselves. Soon they will be shipping fish, furs, and lumber back to England.

Without the Indians they might not have survived. Picture this scene: Pilgrims are struggling to find ways to live in this difficult region, when out of the woods strides a tall man in deerskin clothes. They are astounded when he greets them. "Welcome, Englishmen," he says. His name is Samoset, and he has learned some English from fishermen and traders.

Samoset returns with 60 Indians, a chieftain named Massasoit, and an Indian whom the settlers name Squanto. Squanto speaks English well. He had been kidnapped by sailors, taken to London, befriended by a London merchant, and then returned to his native land.

Trumpet and drums are played as the Pilgrims' governor, John Carver, leads Massasoit to his house, kisses his hand (as is proper to a king), offers refreshments, and writes a treaty of peace between the Indians and the English. While Massasoit is alive, the peace will be kept.

Squanto stays with the settlers. To the Pilgrims he was "a special instrument sent of God for their good beyond their expectation....He directed them how to set [plant] their corn, where to take [catch] fish, and to procure other commodities, and was also their pilot to bring them to unknown places."

Edward Winslow was a printer and a clever man. He traveled a lot to London to trade and negotiate for the Pilgrims. On his first trip back to Plymouth he brought something very important: cattle.

Not all the early colonists dressed in somber styles and colors. Only the Saints insisted on plain, dark clothes.

One of America's first folk songs praised the humble but essential pumpkin.

For pottage and puddings and custards and pies
Our pumpkins and parsnips are common supplies.
We have pumpkin at morning and pumpkin at noon,
If it were not for pumpkin,
We should be undone.

In 1621, after the first harvest, the Pilgrims invite their Indian friends to a three-day feast of Thanksgiving. In one year they have accomplished much.

The Pilgrims are frugal, but the celebration is unusually generous. They will need their food to get through the winter and to help feed the new colonists who are beginning to arrive.

William Bradford, who is elected governor when John Carver dies suddenly, keeps a record of the arrivals. When the ship *Fortune* docks he writes, "there was not so much as biscuit-cake, neither had they any bedding…nor pot, or pan."

Abraham Pearce, a black indentured servant, is one of those who comes in 1623. A few years later he will own land, vote, and be a respected member of the community.

The new arrivals bring reports from England that are not good. Now the Puritans are in trouble. The Puritans are also called Saints, but they are more moderate than the Pilgrims. Remember, Puritans don't want to separate themselves from the Church of England, they want to purify the church. What they really want is to control the Church of England; of course, King James and those in charge don't want that at all.

The Puritans can't stand King James and he doesn't like them either. Of the Puritans he says, "I will make them conform themselves, or else I will harry [harass] them out of the land." The Puritans can see that King James isn't good for England's economy. First there is inflation and then a depression. James has brought his big-spending friends to England from Scotland, where he is also king. They are getting special favors. The Puritans are not.

And so a group of Puritans gathers at Cambridge University, where most of them have gone to college, and makes plans to sail to America. The Puritans are better educated than the Pilgrims—and richer, too. John Winthrop, their leader, is a lawyer, born on a manor, with servants and tenants.

When King James dies, in 1625, and Charles I becomes king, things get even worse for the Puritans.

Edward Winslow wrote this pamphlet to encourage more colonists to come to New England.

Giving Thanks

The story that the first American Thanksgiving was held at Plymouth Colony is a real turkey. In 1540, long before the Pilgrims sat down to their big dinner, Francisco Vasquez de Coronado and his men conducted a thanksgiving service in their camp at Palo Duro Canyon in what is now known as the Texas Panhandle.

Half a century before the Pilgrims landed, French Huguenots settled near today's Jacksonville, Florida. They "sang a psalm of Thanksgiving unto God, beseeching Him...to continue his accustomed goodness toward us." Unfortunately for the French, the goodness did not continue. Their colony was wiped out by Spanish raiders. Still, some Floridians claim that as the first American Thanksgiving.

A group of English Catholics arrived in Maine in 1605, said prayers of thanks, faced a year of Maine weather, changed their minds about living in America, and sailed back to England. But some Mainiacs (yes, that's what they are called) say their state had the first Thanksgiving.

Two years before the feast in Massachusetts, the settlers at Berkeley Hundred, on the James River in Virginia, decreed that the day of their landing, December 4, 1619, "shall be yearly and perpetually kept holy as a day of Thanksgiving." Did they have a feast? It depends on whom you ask at Berkeley Plantation. (There is no documented record of one.)

Now, to give the Pilgrims their due: they did eat a big meal, and one of them—Edward Winslow—wrote six sentences about it. None of the other claimants can say that.

Those Pilgrims needed a good meal. Fewer than half of the 102 passengers who came on the *Mayflower* in 1620 survived their first American winter. The local Indians weren't in good shape either. They had been hit—hard hit—by diseases brought by French fishermen, who had made contact four years earlier.

The English colonists wouldn't have survived at all—and they knew it—if it hadn't been for corn and other help from the Indians. And Massasoit was forever grateful to Winslow, who made a nourishing broth that helped him recover from a serious illness. Good will, necessity, and plain good sense seem to have made them all good neighbors.

So when harvest time arrived in 1621, the Pilgrims had much to be thankful for. They had made a start at the beaver trade, they lived in peace with the Native Americans, 11 houses had been built, and, thanks to Squanto, the corn harvest was good. They had celebrated harvest time in Holland; they wished to continue that tradition.

They invited Massasoit to join them. He came with 90 hungry Indians. They might have wiped out the larder, but the Indians "went and killed five deer, which they brought to the plantation and bestowed on our governor," Winslow writes.

We don't know exactly what the Pilgrims cooked, but ducks, geese, turkey, clams, eels, lobster, squash, wild grapes, dried fruit, and cornbread are all good guesses, along with watercress and other "sallet herbes." Winslow says, "Our governor sent four men on fowling, that so we might after a special manner rejoice together after we had gathered the fruit of our labors. They four in one day killed as much fowl as, with a little help beside, served the company almost a week." That's as detailed as he gets, with this addition: "for three days we entertained and feasted."

That's all we know? That's it. Except for a brief word from Governor William Bradford, who doesn't write specifically about a feast with the Indians, but does say that "they began now to gather in the small harvest they had....All summer there was no want; and now began to come in store of fowl, as winter approached, of which this place did abound....And besides wa-

(continued on p.58)

terfowl there was great store of wild turkeys, of which they took many, besides venison, etc. Besides, they had about a peck of meal a week to a person, or now since harvest, Indian corn in that proportion."

Did they eat cranberries, which were thick in the nearby bogs? Or pumpkin pie? Not likely. You need sugar for those dishes, and they didn't have any.

As devout Christians, the Pilgrims gave thanks before each meal. But this was a harvest festival, not, primarily, a celebration of thanks to God. And it probably came at the end of September. Still, all in all, the spirit was the same as at today's November festival where we give thanks, we remember, we enjoy—and we eat!

The first national Thanksgiving was actually proclaimed by George Washington in 1789. But Thanksgiving was not celebrated officially again until Abraham Lincoln (urged on by a magazine editor, Sarah J. Hale) decreed a national holiday in 1863. Since then it's been turkey all the way.

This is the first Thanksgiving dinner celebrated by the Pilgrims and Native Americans, as pictured by the artist J.L.G. Ferris (1863-1930). No one really knows if they ate outdoors or not.

15 Puritans, Puritans, and More Puritans

Massachusetts is an Algonquian word that means "at the big hill." The Puritans called their new home the Massachusetts Bay Colony.

John Winthrop was a lawyer who lost his job because of his religion. In 1630 he came to America.

In 1630, the first Puritan ship, the *Arbella,* sets out for the New World. By summer's end 1,000 Puritans have landed in New England. They bring a charter from the king: the Charter of the Company of the Massachusetts Bay in New England. King Charles is happy to see the Puritans leave England.

The charter is a document written by lawyers, setting the rules that tell how the colony will be run. It allows the colonists to govern themselves. It is important to remember that, from the beginning, English settlers expected to govern themselves. It is important to remember that each colony had a charter: a written set of rules. Those charters would evolve into constitutions.

Can you guess what might happen in a community without a charter or constitution? Would you like to live in a country without laws? Would you want to write your own laws or have someone write them for you?

You can think about those questions and then get back to the Puritans, who are beginning to pour out of England. Most of them go to the Caribbean islands, where sugar is creating great fortunes. But, between 1630 and 1640, 20,000 Puritans sail for New England. Think about all those people risking their lives to cross the ocean and settle in an unknown land. It is almost as if tens of thousands of people today decided to live in outer space.

Why did they come? Many came because they really cared about their religion and wanted to practice it in peace. They wanted to build a holy community, where people would live by the rules of the Bible. Puritans believed the Bible was the whole word of God. They tried to follow its every direction, which means they tried to live very good lives.

Sweet Success

Sugar was a much-desired luxury in Europe. The West Indies (with its tropical climate) turned out to be a perfect place to grow sugarcane. Christopher Columbus brought the cane to the Caribbean on his second voyage. Soon the native trees were cut down and sugarcane plantations filled the islands.

Sugarcane grew wild in Asia. In Sanskrit, the ancient language of India, sugar was *sarkara*. That became *sukkar* in Arabic, *sakhar* in Russian, *sucre* in French, *Zucker* in German, and *sugar* in English.

Here is the first page of the Charter of the Massachusetts Bay Colony, setting out the rules by which the colonists could govern themselves. At the top left is King William III.

Once a woman got to the New World, she was expected to start having babies—that's what the Puritans on the left are telling the couple to do.

At first, the name *Quaker* was used to make fun of people; so, too, was the word *Puritan*. Then both groups decided to be proud of those words and use them themselves.

Although the Puritans tried hard to be good, things didn't work out as they wished. They expected their colony to be an example for all the world. John Winthrop, who was chosen as governor, said, "We must consider that we shall be as a city upon a hill. The eyes of all people are upon us."

One thing they didn't understand at all was the idea of *toleration*. Puritans came to America to find religious freedom—but only for themselves. They didn't believe in the kind of religious freedom we have today. But don't be too hard on them. Almost no one else believed in it either. And how many people do you know who are willing to devote their lives to an idea they believe to be right?

In those days each nation had its own church, and everyone was expected to pay taxes for its support. Suppose you didn't believe in the ideas of that religion. Too bad. You had to keep quiet, leave the country, go to jail, or maybe get hanged.

Pretend you are a Puritan. You think that yours is the only true religion, so you believe the Reverend John Cotton when he says toleration is "liberty...to tell lies in the name of the Lord."

Since you are convinced that only you Puritans are right, you think it is wrong to let anyone practice another religion. You believe that is helping the devil. You especially dislike Quakers. Your leaders call them a "cursed sect." You use the name *Quaker* to describe religious people who call themselves "Friends." Friends believe that each person has an inner light that leads him to God. People with an inner light do not have to rely on a minister to tell them what is godly. The inner light is available to everyone. This is a highly democratic idea, and most Europeans thought it very dangerous. They were used to kings and priests and ministers. It seemed reasonable to them to persecute Quakers. When Quakers came to New England or Virginia, they were whipped, sent away, and even hanged.

Remember, you are a Puritan and you've left your home and everything you know and love. You've crossed a fierce ocean to live as you wish. You don't want people with strange ideas bothering you. Democracy is another strange idea. "If the people be governors, who shall be governed?" the Reverend Cotton asks. John Winthrop, the beloved Puritan governor, who always tries to do what is best, calls democracy the "meanest [lowest] and worst" form of government.

And yet the Puritans do practice a kind of democracy—but only for male church members. Once a year they form a General Court and vote to elect the governor and council. The General Court is a lot like the House of Burgesses, or Parliament, or Congress.

Some people call the Massachusetts Bay Colony a "theocracy" (thee-OCK-ruh-see), government by church officials in the name of God. But they are wrong. It is not a theocracy. The ministers are the most important people in the colony, but they are not allowed to hold political office. They do not govern. It is a small step toward the idea of the separation of church and state. Someday that idea will be a foundation of American liberty.

At Puritan church services women sat at the back or upstairs. At a Quaker meeting *(above)* everyone sat together.

What's in a Word?

We had better stop and go over some words, otherwise this book will get confusing. You've been reading about democracy and theocracy. Here's an explanation of those ideas, and some others, too.

If you keep reading history you will learn about Abraham Lincoln. He said that democracy was government "of the people, by the people, and for the people." That's a good definition.

Democracy is based on people power. Think of a pyramid with the leader on top and all the people on the bottom. The leader is picked from the bottom row and raised to the top. Power goes from the bottom to the top. You'll see in a minute that in some kinds of government, power goes the other way.

Democracy comes in two varieties: direct democracy and representative democracy.

When you choose someone to vote for you, you have *representative democracy*. The members of the House of Burgesses at Jamestown represented the colonists and made laws for them. Our Congress does the same thing for us today. We live in a representative democracy based on law. We are ruled by laws made by congressmen and congresswomen whom we elect.

Some New England towns have *direct democracy*. All the people in the town get together at a town meeting and vote directly on important issues. No one votes for them.

It is possible, with modern technology, that we will have more direct democracy in the future. We may be able to vote directly for certain laws through our TV sets. However, we will always need representatives who can take the time needed to make decisions on complicated issues.

Autocracy is the opposite of democracy. It is government by a single authority with unlimited power. In autocracies, power starts at the top of the pyramid.

A *dictator* is an autocrat. If a dictator doesn't like you, he can have you killed without consulting anyone or giving you a trial. Autocrats don't have to be bad. There have been a few good ones in history—but only a few. If a dictator is terrible, the people are stuck with him (or her). They have no power—except, sometimes, brute force. In the old days, kings and queens were autocrats. Today they usually share power with a parliament.

A *theocracy* is…if you don't remember that, go back and read the last chapter. Just kidding, you don't have to do that. A theocracy (remember?) is government by a church in the name of God.

An *aristocracy* is government by a small group of privileged people. England was an aristocracy in the 17th century. The king and the landowning aristocrats (who controlled Parliament) ruled.

Hold on. This is tough, and may be a bit boring, but it is important.

Democracy, autocracy, theocracy, and aristocracy are all words that tell you about political power and who has it.

Here are two words that tell about economic or money power: *communism* and *capitalism*.

In a communist country the state owns most of the land and property and shares them with its citizens. (Remember, the word *state* sometimes means "nation." That can be confusing, but that's the way it is.) People don't own their own homes or businesses. They work for the state. Jamestown tried a kind of communist system, and so did Plymouth. Both colonies found that people work harder when they know they can own land or a business. (In the 20th century, Russia and most of Eastern Europe tried and rejected communism.) People often need to be forced to be communists.

In a capitalist country you can own capital: capital is money and property. The United States is a nation that practices capitalism. In a capitalist country goods are distributed through a free market. Capitalism has disadvantages, too: wealth often piles up for a few people, while others don't have enough.

Whew, that's a lot to absorb! Now let's get back to history, which is much more exciting.

Alexis de Tocqueville was a Frenchman who came to the United States in the 19th century. He wrote a book, Democracy in America, *that is still one of the best descriptions of our system ever published.*

16 Of Towns and Schools and Sermons

Women who nagged or talked too much—scolds—were considered a curse in the 17th century and could be made to wear a *scold's bridle*.

At first the New England settlers built their homes behind high fences called "stockades." They were fearful of the unknown—of Indians and animals.

Soon they began spreading out, beyond the fences, into small towns with names like Greenfield, Springfield, and Longmeadow. The names described the land. Many of those early settlements were just a row of houses strung alongside abandoned Indian fields that the English settlers found and took. They lived with Indians as neighbors, although their animals sometimes made that difficult.

The Native Americans hunted animals; they had no horses, cows, sheep, or hogs. The Indians soon discovered that those English grazing animals could destroy their cornfields. In 1653 the people of the town of New Haven agreed to work for 60 days to build fences around fields planted by neighboring Indians. New England's courts ordered colonists to pay the Indians for damage done to their fields by wandering animals.

As the colonists began to prosper, they built towns in America that were something like the villages they left behind in Europe. They were compact, easy to defend, and friendly. Castles and manor houses dominated European towns; in New England's villages it was the meetinghouse that stood out. The meetinghouse was used as a church, a town hall, and a social center. It was usually placed at one end of a big field that was called a common, because everyone used it in common. Sometimes, when there were sheep to chew the field's grass and keep it short and green, the common was called a green. Houses were built around the green. The houses nearest the meet-

People in New England villages were usually friendly and neighborly to each other. They had to be. A family needed the neighbors' help to clear rocks out of a field or raise a barn roof. There was one cowman who looked after everybody's cows. But if a stranger came hanging around with no invitation from a local family, he was chased out of town.

Chairs were rare and costly in the 17th century. This one belonged to Governor Endicott.

63

The Puritans had so many rules and laws that they were often broken. Another popular punishment, especially for scolding women, was the ducking stool. The sinner was tied on and lowered into the stream or village pond.

Puritans liked to give their children names that were reminders of goodness and holiness. Some we still find occasionally, like Constance, Faith, or Hope; and some seem strange: Joy-from-Above, Kill-sin, Fear, Patience, Wrestling-with-the-Devil.

inghouse belonged to the most important people in town: the minister and the church leaders.

Many villages had a stream. The tumbling water of the stream turned a big wheel, and that provided power for the mills where wood was sawed and wheat ground into flour.

As the town grew other buildings were added: a general store, a blacksmith's shop, a furniture maker's shop, a candle maker's.

If the town was large enough, there might be an inn. Almost always there was a school.

The Puritans cared about schooling. By 1636 they had founded Harvard College. It was amazing that they had a college so soon after they arrived, although Harvard did get off to a rocky start. The first teacher beat his students, fed them spoiled meat, and ran off with college money.

Then they got a college president, Henry Dunster. He was so good that students began coming to study with him from Virginia and

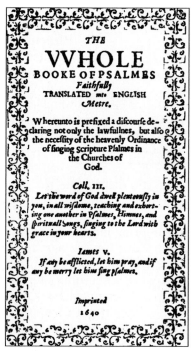

The *Whole Booke of Psalmes*, also known as the Bay Psalm Book, was the first book ever printed in the English colonies.

A footwarmer for churchgoers.

Bermuda and even England itself. Of course, they were all Puritans.

Because of their religion, Puritans weren't allowed to attend college in England. That was one reason it was so important to have Harvard succeed. To do that it had to have a supply of students. So, in 1642, the Massachusetts Bay Colony passed a law saying that parents must teach their children to read.

The Puritans wanted everyone to be able to read the Bible, even those who weren't going to Harvard. So the next thing they did was pass a law that said:

> It is therefore ordered, that every township in this jurisdiction, after the Lord has increased its number to 50 householders, shall then forthwith appoint one within their town to teach all such children as shall resort to him to write and read, whose wages shall be paid either by the parents or masters of such children, or by the inhabitants in general.

In plain English, that means that every town with 50 or more families must have a schoolteacher.

Do you see something unusual in that law? Read that bit at the end, "shall be paid…by the inhabitants in general." Do you know what that means? It means that everyone in the town has to pay for the education of the children. Not just the parents. That is what public education is all about. It guarantees that every child, not just those with wealthy parents, can go to school. In America, it all began with that school law in 1647.

I know what you're thinking. Why did they have to go and do it? Who needs school anyway? But you don't really mean it. It isn't fun to be ignorant.

In the 17th century much teaching was done by parents, or in church, or, if you were an apprentice, by your master. But the Puritans could see that sometimes that wasn't enough. Some parents just weren't good teachers, even though many Puritans were highly educated themselves. The Puritans thought it important that everyone read the Bible. In Boston and the larger towns some children were ac-

Harvard College *(above)* had a very English class consciousness for many years. Until 1769 the roster of students was not listed in alphabetical order, but according to social status. That meant that if you were from an important family, you were listed ahead of somebody of lowly rank.

Several generations learned their ABCs from the *New England Primer (right)*, which used rhymes to help children remember letters. This might be all you got if you were a girl—very few had as much schooling as boys.

tually taught to read the Bible in its original languages. So little Puritan boys and girls of six and seven learned to read Latin and Greek, and a few learned Hebrew, too. That sounds hard, and it was, but learning languages is good training for the mind. Many of this nation's greatest thinkers came from Puritan stock.

Try and take yourself back to Puritan times, and see what you think of Sunday churchgoing. Those Puritan ministers gave sermons that lasted for hours and hours. Sometimes there was an intermission for lunch, and then everyone went back to hear more. There was no heat in the meetinghouse, and New England can get very cold. People brought warming boxes with hot coals in them to keep their feet from freezing. Sometimes they brought their dogs to church for the same reason.

A church official held a tickling rod to wake up anyone who looked as if he might be falling asleep. The dog whipper took out dogs who barked. If you were a troublemaker and wiggled and made noise you could get locked up in the town stocks. You'd have to sit there with your hands and feet stuck into a wooden contraption and everyone would make fun of you.

We know you wouldn't like that kind of life, but maybe things weren't so bad for the Puritan boys and girls. Maybe some of them even looked forward to the sermons. Remember, in Puritan Massachusetts there were no movies and no TVs. At first, there were no newspapers, no magazines, and only a few books. The Puritans were intelligent people who could read and think well. Maybe that will help you understand why everyone tried to listen to the weekly sermon and why Puritans sometimes spent all week talking about it.

Feeling Blue

Rules banning work, trade, and playing on Sundays—the Sabbath—are still called "blue laws," because the Puritans wrote the laws in books bound in blue paper. You could be fined or punished for doing these things on Sunday: running, cooking, making a bed, or shaving. A man was whipped for saying that the minister's sermon was boring. Another was put in the stocks after kissing his wife on his return home from three years at sea. And celebrating Christmas was forbidden. It was "popish"—something that Roman Catholics did. Most Puritans worked on Christmas—unless, of course, it happened to fall on a Sunday.

A · In *Adam's* Fall
We Sinned all.

B · Thy Life to Mend
This *Book* Attend.

C · The *Cat* doth play
And after slay.

D · A *Dog* will bite
A Thief at night.

E · An *Eagles* flight
Is out of sight.

F · The Idle *Fool*
Is whipt at School.

G · As runs the *Glass*
Mans life doth pass.

H · My *Book* and *Heart*
Shall never part.

J · *Job* feels the Rod
Yet blesses GOD.

K · Our *KING* the good
No man of blood.

L · The *Lion* bold
The *Lamb* doth hold.

M · The *Moon* gives light
In time of night.

N · *Nightingales* sing
In Time of Spring.

O · The *Royal Oak*
it was the Tree
That sav'd His
Royal Majestie.

P · *Peter* denies
His Lord and cries.

Q · Queen *Esther* comes
in Royal State
To Save the JEWS
from dismal Fate.

R · *Rachel* doth mourn
For her first born.

S · *Samuel* anoints
Whom God appoints.

T · *Time* cuts down all
Both great and small.

U · *Uriah's* beauteous Wife
Made *David* seek his
Life.

W · *Whales* in the Sea
God's Voice obey.

17 Roger Williams

A KEY into the
LANGUAGE
OF
AMERICA:
OR,
An help to the *Language* of the *Natives*
in that part of A M E R I C A, called
NEW-ENGLAND.

Together, with briefe *Observations* of the Cu-
stomes, Manners and Worships, &c. of the
aforesaid *Natives*, in Peace and Warre,
in Life and Death.

On all which are added Spirituall *Observations,*
Generall and Particular by the *Authour,* of
chiefe and speciall use (upon all occasions,) to
all the *English* Inhabiting those parts ;
yet pleasant and profitable to
the view of all men :

BY ROGER WILLIAMS
of Providence in *New-England.*

LONDON,
Printed by *Gregory Dexter*, 1643.

**The first words Williams
translated in his guide
to the Narraganset lan-
guage were *I love you.***

The Puritans, who were victims of intolerance
in England, were not tolerant themselves.
Although they preached the Golden Rule—do
unto others as you would have them do unto
you—most never understood that they were
breaking that rule. Roger Williams did.

Williams was a Puritan minister who came
to Massachusetts seeking a "pure" religious
community. Like the other Puritans, he was a
serious Christian. Like the others, he disap-
proved of Catholic and Quaker ideas. Like the others, he thought
the Indian religions were pagan.

But that's where "like the others" stops.

He didn't believe in forcing anyone to believe as he did. He believed that killing or punishing in the name of Christianity was sinful. He thought that church members—not general taxes—should
pay the bills at each church. He respected the beliefs of others.
Those were strange ideas in 17th-century Massachusetts.

The Puritans didn't know what to do with Roger Williams. He was
a Puritan, he was brilliant, he was a minister, and he was so nice
that even his opponents had a hard time disliking him.

But what an ungrateful young man he seemed! The Puritans had
offered him good jobs, as teacher and minister, and he thanked
them by criticizing their practices.

Governor Winthrop was shocked. So was John Cotton, the minister who took a job that Williams refused. They were especially
shocked when Williams wrote a book saying it was wrong to persecute people for their beliefs. Williams called his book *The Bloody
Tenet.* (The blood was from those killed because of their religious
ideas.) John Cotton wrote his own book. He called it *The Bloody*

Catholics, Quakers,
and Quakers were all
Christians, but they each
interpreted Christianity in
a different way. To the
Puritans—and to most
Christians—pagan reli-
gions were not "real" religions, as Christianity was.

Tenet Washed and Made White. Of course that didn't end it. Williams's next book was *The Bloody Tenet Made Yet More Bloody by Mr. Cotton's Endeavor to Wash It White in the Blood of the Lamb.*

When Roger Williams started preaching that land shouldn't be taken from the Indians—that the king had no right to charter land that didn't belong to him—that was too much. The officers of the Massachusetts Bay Colony made arrangements to ship Williams back to England. They sent armed men to put him on a boat.

Roger Williams's wife heard the verdict of the court—that he was to be arrested and banished—and began to cry. Williams told her, "Fifty good men did what they thought was just." Roger Williams didn't hold grudges.

But he wasn't about to let himself get shipped back to England, and so he fled from Massachusetts. It was January 1636, he was sick, and the weather was freezing. Later, when he was an old man, Roger Williams would still remember that terrible winter. He was always thankful to the Narraganset Indians, who helped him survive the cold. He learned to love them as they loved him.

He bought land from the Indians and started a colony called Providence. It became the capital of Rhode Island and soon attracted many of those who were not wanted elsewhere. Someone described Providence as the place where "all the cranks of New England" go.

There were plenty of cranks in Providence. But there were also many who were searching for what Williams called "freedom of conscience."

When Roger Williams said *freedom of conscience,* he meant the freedom of each person to follow his own mind and heart and choose his own religion. That was to become an important right in America.

Roger Williams welcomed everyone who wished to come to Rhode Island, including Quakers and Catholics. And, while he continued to disagree with those religions, he never let that stop him from liking some of the people who practiced them. Jews, who were often persecuted elsewhere, were welcome in Rhode Island. Atheists were welcome, too.

Williams believed that state governments should not have any connection with a church. We call that

In 1763, thanks to the atmosphere of tolerance that Roger Williams fostered, Rhode Island became the home of the first permanent Jewish house of worship in America, the Touro Synagogue.

John Cotton *(above)* and most Puritans thought Williams's ideas of toleration were wrong. Maybe they thought he was crazy, too.

A *tenet* (TEN-it) is a basic idea, a fundamental concept. *Atheists* believe there is no God.

69

The poet means "meat" when he says **flesh**. When he says **they part to friends**, he means "they share with friends." He means "to lack humanity" when he says **to want humanity**. Languages keep changing, and some English words were different in the 17th century.

separation of church and state. It was a very new idea at the time.

He knew that people could be forced to go to church, but that no one's mind could be forced to believe. "Forced worship stinks in God's nostrils," said Roger Williams.

He learned the language of the Narraganset Indians and wrote a book so that others could learn it, too. In it he included these rhymes about the Indians:

> *Sometimes God gives them fish or flesh,*
> *Yet they're content without.*
> *And what comes in, they part to friends*
> *And strangers round about.*

> *If nature's sons both wild and tame*
> *Humane and courteous be,*
> *How ill becomes its sons of God*
> *To want humanity!*

When the great Narraganset chief Canonicus (kuh-NON-ih-kuss) was dying, he called for Roger Williams to be with him. White men had destroyed the Indian chief's kingdom, and he hated most of them. But Williams and Canonicus had something in common. Each was able to judge people by their character, not by their skin color or religion. They loved and respected each other.

Edmund S. Morgan, who wrote a book about Roger Williams, said "We may praise him...for his defense of religious liberty and the separation of church and state. He deserves the tribute...but it falls short of the man. His greatness was simpler. He dared to think."

Roger Williams

Church and State

The Puritans forced some Indians to become Christians. Roger Williams wrote a letter to the Massachusetts governor. "Are not the English of this land generally a persecuted people from their native land?" he asked. How could those who had been persecuted persecute others, he wondered? He said that the Indians should "not be forced from their religions."

Roger Williams didn't think anyone should be compelled to follow a religion. Besides, he knew it never works to try that. You can make people do things, but you can't make them believe what they don't want to believe.

Williams said that it was "against the testimony of Christ Jesus for the civil state to impose [force] upon the souls of the people a religion."

Most Puritans didn't agree with Roger Williams. They thought it was the job of the government leaders to tell people what to believe.

But Roger Williams's ideas won out. They helped bring about the separation of church and state that is one of the most important of all of America's governing ideas. In Europe and the rest of the world, millions of people have died in wars over religion, but that has not happened in this country.

Roger Williams, a devout Puritan, wrote, "Jesus never called for the sword of steel to help the sword of spirit."

18 "Woman, Hold Your Tongue"

Anne Hutchinson's clothes were plainer than these. But still she had to wear underskirts and petticoats. Imagine wash day, and no washing machine.

From Me to Thee

Puritans and Quakers used the words *thou* and *thee* instead of "you," and *thy* and *thine* instead of "your" and "yours." They are old-fashioned words that people used when talking to a child, a close friend or family member, a servant—or God. What the Puritans were saying with those words was that we are all close; we are all brothers and sisters.

No More Diapers

You might think that Anne Hutchinson had a terrible lot of diapers to change with all those children. But as soon as a baby could sit up its tight swaddling bands were taken off. In warm rooms and climates, babies didn't wear anything—though sometimes a mother wrapped a "baby clout" (probably just a piece of linen) around a baby's bottom when it sat on somebody's lap. In colder weather, babies and little kids mostly just wore a shirt—with nothing underneath. When toddlers had to go to the bathroom, their mothers plunked them down outside. Not very hygienic, maybe, but simple.

Anne Hutchinson was another troublemaker. At least that is what some Puritans thought. Here was a woman with 14 children who was interpreting the Bible. No one objected to that, until she began to question some of the ministers' beliefs. Soon she was trying to reach everyone with her ideas about God. Governor Winthrop was outraged. Didn't Mistress Hutchinson have enough to do, with all those babies to feed?

What was worse, in Winthrop's view, was that people were listening to her. Even men were listening. There was a reason: Anne Hutchinson had a fine mind, and she loved God. Besides, what she was saying made sense. Winthrop admitted that she was "a woman with a ready wit and bold spirit." Before long, Massachusetts was split between people who believed what Anne Hutchinson said and those who believed the ministers. She claimed God was guiding her; the ministers said they were doing God's work on earth.

Finally, the Puritans held a trial. You can read the court records for yourself. You may agree that Mrs. Hutchinson was smarter than her accusers, but that didn't help her a bit. She was kicked out of Massachusetts and out of the Puritan church, too. She moved to Rhode Island. Later Anne Hutchinson moved to New York and was killed by Indians. Governor Winthrop saw it as the judgment of God.

In those days, women, like children, were expected to be seen but not heard. They belonged to their husbands. The word for them

Marbury Scott had enough of life in Massachusetts after the trial and exile of her sister Ann Marbury Hutchinson, so she decided to move with her family to Rhode Island. Twenty years later, "a grave, sober, ancient woman," she returned to protest when the Puritans punished another Quaker named Christopher Holder by cutting off his ear. The Puritans imprisoned her, had her whipped with a "threefold corded knotted whip," and threatened to kill her should she return again. She said: "If God calls us, woe be to us if we come not, but He whom we love will make us not to count our lives dear unto ourselves for the sake of his name." Governor John Endicott replied: "And we shall be as ready to take away your lives as ye shall be to lay them down."

was *chattel.* That means a "piece of property." A husband could sell his wife's labor and keep the wages. If she ran away, she was accused of stealing herself and her clothing. Her husband even owned her clothes.

Female Power in Massachusetts

In 1649 and 1650, six petitions—all from Massachusetts women—were submitted to the magistrates on behalf of a midwife named Alice Tilley (midwives deliver babies). Tilley had been accused and convicted—by the male authorities—of some kind of medical malpractice (no exact account survives). Four of the women's petitions asked that Mistress Tilley be allowed to leave jail to tend her patients. Two asked that "her innocencie may be cleared."

According to historian Mary Beth Norton, "female Bostonians begged the judges to "heare the cryes of mothers, and of children yet unborn." They wanted Tilley to deliver babies. "The astonishing aspect of the petitions," says Norton, "was the total number of signatures (294)." The women won; Alice Tilley was released from prison and presumably went back to work.

From a Massachusetts Court Record, 1637

ANNE HUTCHINSON: Therefore take heed how you proceed against me, for I know that for this you go about to do me, God will ruin you and your posterity, and this whole state.

MR. NOWELL: How do you know that it was God that did reveal these things to you, and not Satan?

MRS. HUTCHINSON: How did Abraham know that it was God that bid him offer [sacrifice] his son, being a breach of the sixth commandment?

DEPUTY-GOVERNOR DUDLEY: By an immediate voice.

MRS. HUTCHINSON: So to me by an immediate revelation.

DEPUTY-GOVERNOR: How! an immediate revelation?

MRS. HUTCHINSON: By the voice of his own spirit to my soul.

GOVERNOR JOHN WINTHROP: Daniel was delivered by miracle; do you think to be delivered so too?

MRS. HUTCHINSON: I do here speak it before the Court. I look that the Lord should deliver me by his providence....

GOVERNOR WINTHROP: The Court hath already declared themselves satisfied concerning the things you hear, and concerning the troublesomeness of her spirit, and the danger of her course amongst us, which is not to be suffered. Therefore, if it be the mind of the Court that Mrs. Hutchinson, for these things that appear before us, is unfit for our society, and if it be the mind of the Court that she shall be banished out of our liberties, and imprisoned till she be sent away, let them hold up their hands.

All but three held up their hands.

GOVERNOR WINTHROP: Those that are contrary minded, hold up yours.

Mr. Coddington and Mr. Colburn only.

MR. JENNISON: I cannot hold up my hand one way or the other, and I shall give my reason if the Court require it.

GOVERNOR WINTHROP: Mrs. Hutchinson, you hear the sentence of the Court. It is that you are banished from out our jurisdiction as being a woman not fit for our society. And you are to be imprisoned till the Court send you away.

MRS. HUTCHINSON: I desire to know wherefore [why] I am banished.

GOVERNOR WINTHROP: Say no more. The Court knows wherefore, and is satisfied.

Here's a Pilgrim house that you can visit at Plimoth Plantation in Massachusetts. There you will see a whole village reconstructed to seem just as if it were 1627. Big open hearths like this were the center of every Pilgrim home.

A Home for Prayer

Religious fervor also swept through parts of Germany in the 17th century, and some of these people—who were often considered bizarre in the Old World—headed across the ocean to search for a home where they could be free to follow their beliefs. One such group was called "The Woman in the Wilderness." (The *woman* was the true church.) Johannes Kelpius was its leader, and he settled near Philadelphia and built a big, log-walled monastery to house his 40 fellow worshipers. There they studied mystical writings, engaged in devout meditation, conducted scientific experiments—which they hoped would prolong their lives indefinitely—and put a telescope on their roof to search for signs of God's arrival. Members of a number of sects sought salvation on American soil. Massachusetts already had its Puritans, and most of them didn't encourage other beliefs. So Pennsylvania was where many German religious groups headed.

19 Statues on the Common

This Quaker was arrested for preaching, driven out of town, and beaten with a cat-o'-nine-tails.

At Quaker meetings, the congregation sits and meditates in silence. Sometimes a member feels that God is communicating with him or her directly. The Friend might start talking aloud about this "inward light," or might shake and tremble—which was how the Quakers got their name.

Anne Hutchinson wasn't the only strong woman to trouble John Winthrop and the Massachusetts Bay Puritans. Her best friend was a problem, too.

Mary Dyer was Puritan and pious. Winthrop called her a "very proper and fair woman." That was when he first knew her. But Dyer followed the ways of Anne Hutchinson, and when Anne Hutchinson was cast out of Massachusetts, Mary Dyer and her husband, William, and other believers went with her.

Later, Mary Dyer took a trip back to England and found other truths for herself. She became a member of the Society of Friends, the people who were known as Quakers. Quakers call their church services "meetings." In a Quaker meeting everyone is equal, anyone may speak out, and there are no ministers. Now, in the 17th century equality was not fashionable. Besides, Quakers refuse to swear oaths of allegiance to anyone but God. But oaths of loyalty to king and country were expected in England and everywhere in the 17th century.

You need to understand that the church and the government were all part of one package in the Old World. It was the church

At this Quaker meeting most of the congregation sits in silent meditation while one member is inspired to speak.

that gave the king his right to govern. It was called the "divine right of kings." It was the government that gave the church support and lands. That was the way it had always been. It seemed as if people like the Quakers wanted to mess things up. The Quakers believed in toleration, and they believed each person could think for himself. What happens if you let people think for themselves? Why, the next step might be for them to say that the king's church and the king's priests weren't needed. And Quakers did say something like that when they sat in their meetings without ministers.

A hanging, like that of Mary Dyer, was a public spectacle in the 17th century. People took time off work to go and watch. They cheered, jeered, and partied.

So maybe you can see why Quakers were hated and persecuted by the authorities in England. They weren't liked any better in the colonies. The magistrates of the Massachusetts Bay Colony passed harsh laws to keep them away, but that didn't stop them. Some Quakers seemed determined to be martyrs, and Mary Dyer was one of them. She came to Boston and was sent away. She came back. This time she was tried, with two Quaker men, and all three were led to the gallows.

The men were hanged, but at the last minute Dyer was put on a horse and sent off to Rhode Island. She came back again. Now what do you do with a woman who cares so much about her religion that she will risk death to preach its message? You'd think the Puritans would have understood that devotion. Maybe they did, and that's what scared them.

The Puritans tried Mary Dyer again. This time they offered her her life if she would leave Massachusetts forever. She refused. Mary Dyer was hanged, on June 1, 1660, on the Boston Common in front of where the State House stands today. Her death was too much for some Puritans. In 1661 the law was changed. Today, statues of Mary Dyer and Anne Hutchinson can be seen on the Common.

A *martyr* (MAR-tur) is someone who would rather die than give up his or her belief. A *gallows* was the two standing poles and crosspiece from which people were hanged. Sometimes bodies were left on the gallows for a while, as a warning to others.

But most Puritans thought they had done everything they could to be fair to Mary Dyer. Remember, it was a different world then, a world just leaving the Middle Ages. A few people in Europe were beginning to question the old ideas. But those questions traveled slowly across the ocean. When people started talking of toleration, the Puritans "could hardly understand what was happening in the world," writes Perry Miller, a historian of the Puritans. "They could not for a long time be persuaded that they had any reason to be ashamed of their record of so many Quakers whipped, blasphemers punished by the amputation of ears, [dissenters] exiled...or witches executed. [According to the beliefs] in Europe at the time the Puritans had left, these were achievements to which any government could point with pride."

20 Of Witches and Dinosaurs

Everybody believed in witches. James I wrote a book that said they should be put to death.

That phrase, *city upon a hill,* is one to put in your head and remember. You'll hear it again and again when you read American history.

How many Puritans do you know? Don't think too hard. The answer is zero. Puritans are like dinosaurs: they are extinct.

I'll tell you what happened to them in just a minute, but don't worry, things worked out well. Many of their descendants turned into New England Yankees. Others are spread all across the nation. Many go to the Congregational church. In some ways, however, we are all descendants of the Puritans.

Now you may be shaking your head if you live in California, or Colorado, or West Virginia. If your parents came from Mexico or China, you're probably saying, "No way am I a Puritan!" But it's true. If you are an American, you are a descendant of the Puritans—at least a little bit—because many American laws and ideas come from Puritan laws and ideas, and they are some of the best we have.

You see, the Puritans hoped to build a place on earth where people could live as the Bible says they should, a place where people would be truly good. Governor Winthrop called Puritan Massachusetts "a city upon a hill." He expected it to stand tall as a symbol to the rest of the world. "The eyes of all people are upon us," he said.

The Puritans came to the New World to try and build a godly community where they could live close to perfect lives. No human beings have ever been able to do that, but the Puritans tried.

To make their community pure, the Puritans

Do you know of other societies or times in history where neighbors spy on neighbors—sometimes, even, where children spy on their parents?

Matthew Hopkins, England's Witch Finder General.

expected everyone to act like a spy and report any neighbor who did or said anything wrong. Can you see how that might make you a little uncomfortable around your neighbors? Maybe that helped cause the Puritans' downfall. Or perhaps it was their seriousness that did them in, or witches (we'll get to them soon), or their self-righteousness.

Self-righteous people believe they know the truth. They think that anyone who doesn't agree with them is wrong. They are apt to judge other people. Sometimes the Puritans were like that. They spent time judging their neighbors.

They read the Bible every day, but they didn't always pay attention to the passage in the New Testament that asks: "Why do you observe the speck of sawdust in your brother's eye and never notice the log in your own?" (What does that mean?)

A witch and her imps. An imp could be a monster, but more often it was an ordinary animal—even a fish—with horns or wings.

Benjamin Franklin, one of the wisest of all Americans, wrote in his *Autobiography* a warning against using words like "certainly, undoubtedly, or any others that give the air of positiveness to an opinion." Instead, said Franklin, we should say, "it appears to me, or I should think it so or so...if I am not mistaken."

The Puritans were very sure of themselves. They believed that God saves only a very few people and that the rest go to a terrible hell filled with fires. They thought that God decided when a child was born if he was saved or not. They used the word "elected" instead of saved, and they thought they were God's elect. Because of that, they thought they should act like God's elect and lead good lives. And that's why we can be happy they were among the first colonists. They really tried their best to be good. They worked hard, they believed in learning, and they did what they thought was right.

Witch Advice

If the cream won't turn to butter, a witch must be in the churn. Take a horse-shoe, heat it red hot, and throw it into the churn. That will set the witch flying.

Nail a horseshoe over your door, and witches will stay away.

To tell if someone is a witch: tie the suspect's hands and feet. Toss him (or her) in the water. If he sinks he is innocent. If he floats he is a witch. (Which would you rather be?)

No one made pictures of the Salem witch trials while they were happening, so we can only imagine what they were like from what was written down. This artist imagined the trial of George Jacobs, the old man kneeling on the right. (Men could be witches, too.)

But the Puritans had a big problem. They were human and they made mistakes. Their ministers didn't help. The ministers said that people were naturally sinful, but if they sinned they would go to that terrible hell. That kept everyone under constant pressure to be close to perfect. No one could relax. And that may be what caused the nightmare of the witches.

The whole world believed in witches—there was nothing new about that. People thought that if you wanted to make a bargain with the devil you could do it, and then torment people and fly through the air on a broomstick, or become invisible and squeeze through keyholes. Everyone *knew* that witches could create thunder, sink ships, kill sheep, and make tables and chairs rattle.

Back in the days of Christopher Columbus, Pope Innocent VIII had issued orders that witches were to be burned. So in Switzerland, during three months in 1515, more than 500 witches went to the stake. Soon fires were lit in France and Germany and all over Europe. England's King James wrote a book about witches, but he wasn't alone. London's publishers were busy with the subject. In the 17th

Judge Samuel Sewall sentenced several witches to death. Later he apologized.

century, Parliament appointed Matthew Hopkins as witch finder. And Hopkins found a lot of witches. Anyone with a pimple or a wart or a mole was a suspect. Those were said to be devil's marks. It was amazing—after torture, many people confessed to knowing the devil.

In the colonies some men and women were hanged or drowned for witchery, but what happened in Salem, Massachusetts, was different from the usual story.

It all began with some little girls and their servant, Tituba. Now Tituba was a poor woman from the West Indies who told stories of the devil and witches and voodoo. The girls were nine-year-old Elizabeth Parris, eleven-year-old Abigail Williams, and their friends. Tituba's stories must have been scary, especially around the fire at night. But when Tituba taught the girls to bark like dogs and mew like cats and grunt like hogs, that might have been fun. Although Elizabeth's father, the Reverend Samuel Parris, didn't think it was fun at all. When he saw the children grunting and mewing and sometimes acting as if they were having fits or spasms, he remembered reading books from England about spells laid on people by witches. He became alarmed.

And then, to everyone's astonishment, on Sunday the girls spoke out during church meeting and said silly things. "There is a yellow bird on the minister's

Four witches are hanged in this 1655 picture. That is the hangman on the ladder. The man on the right is the witch finder, taking his money.

head," cried Anne Putnam. No one would interrupt a church service except the devil! So when the girls said Sarah Good, Sarah Osburn, and Tituba were bewitching them, everyone believed them. The two Sarahs denied the charge. But they were old and poor and no one listened to them, especially after Tituba said that she did indeed fly through the air on a broomstick.

The little girls might have been pretending when they started,

Evil Explained

It wasn't only people from European cultures who feared witches or killed people suspected of witchcraft. Some Native Americans did the same thing. It happened among people who—like the Puritans—were very religious, and wanted an answer to an overwhelming question.

If God is good, how do you explain evil? That is the big question that has concerned people from the beginning of time. It is a central question of great literature and philosophy and religions in all cultures.

There is an easy answer: witches. Suppose you can't explain a sudden earthquake that destroys your town. Suppose you can't explain a disease that kills the young and sweet and promising. Suppose you can't explain a blight that settles on the corn crop and destroys your winter food supply.

Witchcraft is the easy answer. Like the Puritans, the Indians of the pueblo explained the unexplainable with witches. In times of crisis they accused some among themselves of witchcraft, and then they killed the accused. Sometimes one or two witches were enough. Sometimes, as at Salem, it took as many as 20 to exhaust the people's fear.

The Reverend Cotton Mather was a minister and a member of one of Puritan New England's most important families. He was a scholar, and one of the first Americans to promote the smallpox vaccine when most thought it dangerous. Yet he believed firmly in witches and encouraged the hysteria in Salem.

but soon they were telling of torture and witchery, and perhaps they convinced themselves. (Or maybe, now, they were afraid to tell the truth.) Their stories grew longer and their screeches louder. They accused one person after another of putting spells on them. People came from all over Massachusetts to watch them squeal and grunt. What was to be done? Suddenly, anything that went wrong in that little town was the fault of a witch. Salem was mad with witch fever. Five-year-old Dorcas Good was taken to jail and chained to her mother when the girls said she was tormenting them. Then other people began talking of witches and pointing at their neighbors. A court was called to hear the evidence. The judges were scared, like everyone else. The leaders of the community, who might have done some thinking, didn't. More than 100 people were tried as witches; 20 people and two dogs were put to death. Then the Reverend Hale's wife was accused. But there was no one in Massachusetts more beloved and godly than she! Could it be that the girls were wrong? Everyone had believed them; no one had believed the victims. Were those people who had been killed innocent? Yes, an awful tragedy had occurred.

The witch trials were a shameful chapter in American history, although when one of the judges, Samuel Sewall, realized the wrong that had been done, he publicly apologized. The court cleared the names of those who had died. That does make this story better than some. It was a time of witch fear. There had been many witch hangings and burnings in Europe and America; never before was there a public apology. But something devilish did die in that little town of Salem. It was the belief in witchcraft. Most people had learned a sad lesson.

Some Hard Questions

The Puritans have a bad image today. People think of them as narrow bigots. That's not quite fair. The Puritans were sophisticated, sincere believers who thought they had found the truth. They were people who wanted to do right in what they saw as an evil world. The Puritans had left Europe because they didn't want their children tempted by worldly society. But that society followed them. There was to be no escape from the real world.

The problem—for people who believed they knew the ultimate truth—was how to react when their "truths" seemed wrong.

The witchcraft crisis was a problem. So were the hanging of Mary Dyer, the expulsion of Roger Williams, and the persecution of countless Puritans who were thought to have "sinned." Their children and grandchildren began asking questions for which there were no good answers. The old religion was not to survive in the new land.

21 Connecticut, New Hampshire, and Maine

The New Haven colonists made their own rules. One said that every male had to have his hair "cut round."

No one is ever all bad or all good. The witch trials may have been a low point for the Puritans, but mostly these were good, strong, intelligent people. If they hadn't been, they never would have crossed the ocean; they would have stayed in England, as most English people did—even when they didn't like the way they were ruled.

Because the Puritans were independent thinkers they sometimes disagreed with each other. When they did, there was plenty of room in America. They could just start a new settlement.

Thomas Hooker was minister in a little town near Boston when, in 1636, he decided to move west; 100 of his followers went with him. He went to the beautiful valley of the Connecticut River. Today, no one is quite sure if he moved because of religious disagreements, or because the valley was fertile and farming was easier than in rocky Massachusetts. Perhaps it doesn't matter. He found good farmland and he was free to preach as he wished.

Hooker had no charter when he arrived in Connecticut. The king hadn't given him permission to be there. He moved in anyway. He had no legal right to the land in the eyes of the English (and certainly none in the eyes of the Native Americans), so the Connecticut settlers sent their governor, John Winthrop II, to England to get a charter.

When he went to see King Charles II, Winthrop wore a handsome ring that had belonged to Anne of Denmark, who happened to be Charles's grandmother. Winthrop gave the ring to Charles. The king, naturally, was delighted to have his grandmother's ring.

An artist's idea of the emigration of Rev. Hooker and his followers to Connecticut. Mrs. Hooker is in a litter—which was like a covered bed with poles to carry it by.

WHALING

and FISHING

TURKEY and DEER

FOR PUNISHMENT *The Pillary*

MAKING SOAP

COOKING UTENSILS

SHIP-BUILDING

FIRST MEETING HOUSE
New Haven

CLAIMED BY N.Y. and N.H.

MAINE
PART OF MASSACHUSETTS

NEW HAMPSHIRE

Connecticut R.

Merrimack R.

ATLANTIC OCEAN

Deerfield

MASSACHUSETTS

Salem
Boston

Plymouth

Hudson R.

Hartford   Providence

CONNECTICUT

New Haven   New London

CAPE COD

RHODE ISLAND

The NEW ENGLAND COLONIES

Connecticut got a charter. The land it granted stretched as far west as the Pacific Ocean (although no one knew how far that was)!

Soon Puritans were heading straight for Connecticut. Massachusetts was getting crowded and the land in Connecticut was inviting. A group settled at New Haven in 1638 and another at New London in 1646. Each town had its own minister. The New Haven colonists published a list of laws that said how you were to behave. One law said "Every male shall have his hair cut round." Another said, "Married persons must live together, or be imprisoned."

In 1639, the settlers in the Connecticut River colony had an open meeting in which they drafted a groundbreaking document known as the Fundamental Orders. It was a constitution establishing a democratic state controlled by "substantial" citizens.

While all this was going on, some people were moving north. The king had given a big piece of northern land to two friends: John Mason and Ferdinano Gorges. They divided that land: Gorges taking what became Maine, and Mason taking New Hampshire.

Mason and Gorges advertised for settlers in England, and people came.

At first, New Hampshire was part of Massachusetts, with John Mason as its proprietor. Then it became a separate colony; finally the king took it back and held it himself as a royal colony.

Maine was never a separate colony; it was part of Massachusetts until 1820, when it became the 23rd state.

As soon as colonies were established, they began competing for good land and good people. The more people who came, the more land they needed.

The big losers in this contest were the Indians. Serious colonization could not take place until the Indians had been pushed off the land. And pushed off they would be.

Mapmaker Hugo Allard drew this colorful map in 1673 to celebrate the Dutch claim to New Netherland. He got a bit carried away, and included the whole coast from Maine to Virginia.

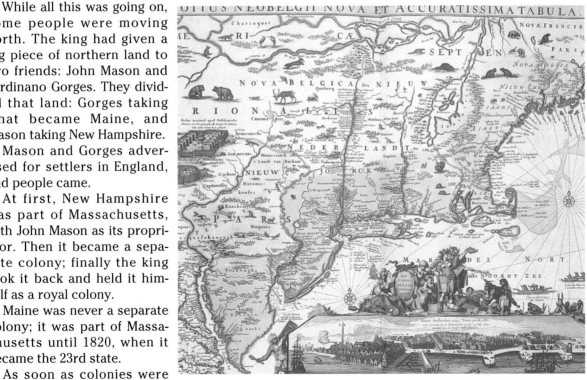

John Mason named New Hampshire after the county of Hampshire, which is on England's south coast.

Land Greed

It was the land that confused the Europeans—there was so much of it. They didn't know how to react. In Europe only the really wealthy—the aristocrats—could own land. Ordinary people didn't even dream of their own land. In America the land was so vast it would take the Europeans more than 200 years just to know how much there was. For a very long time, almost every free person who came to America could afford land.

Most Europeans couldn't quite believe their good fortune. They brought Europe's land greed with them. Each of them wanted to own land—often more than he needed. And almost as soon as the European-Americans got land, they wanted to change it, as Europe's land had been changed.

And so they looked at the beautiful forests and saw an enemy that needed conquering. And they conquered. They cut down trees, leveled hills, filled in swamps, and killed animals and birds. They didn't understand how to work with nature, as the Indians often did. They forced nature to conform to their ways and wants.

It turned out that the land wasn't endless, as they seemed to think at first. One day it would almost all be tamed. Then they would wish for some of those thick forests, some of those songbirds, some of the native animals.

There would be few of them left.

The Indians didn't accept the European idea of landownership. Their religions taught them that the land and waters and animals belonged to God. They thought land could only be shared, not owned. So at first, when they signed treaties selling land, they thought they were selling the right to share it. They didn't expect to be ordered off the land.

Their beliefs told them to live in harmony with nature. Land was to be used by a tribe as a whole, not owned by individuals. It was a way of looking at the land that did away with most greed, but not all greed. Tribes often fought each other for control of the use of land.

Of course, if large numbers of people were to live on the land it had to be changed. Millions and millions of people can't live in a forest. Cities were needed for all the people who would come to live on this bountiful land. And so we built cities and suburbs and in the process often polluted and burned and destroyed. Did we have to do that? Can we have cities and also sheltering woodlands and clean rivers and abundant wildlife? Yes, but it isn't easy. We have to care about our environment. We have to respect the natural world.

Some say one answer is to put heavy industry on space platforms. Some say high-speed trains can be put underground. Some say ideas in science-fiction books can become fact and make the environment healthier.

Can you do anything to help? Of course you can. Do you throw trash around? Does your family worry about pollution? Have you ever helped clean up your neighborhood? Do you know what *conservation* means?

This View Towards Canaan and Salisbury in Connecticut *was made in 1789, but it conveys that feeling of the early settlers—that the land in America went on forever.*

22 King Philip's War

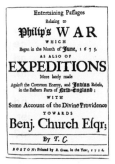

Entertaining Paſſages
Relating to
Philip's WAR
WHICH
Begun in the Month of **June**, 1 6 7 5.
AS ALSO OF
EXPEDITIONS
More lately made
Againſt the Common Enemy, and **Indian Rebels,**
in the Eaſtern Parts of **New-England** :
WITH
Some Account of the Divine Providence
TOWARDS
Benj. Church Eſqr;
By *T. C*
BOSTON: Printed by B. Green, in the Year, 1 7 1 6.

The "entertaining" memoirs of Benjamin Church, who led colonial forces against King Philip.

Many settlers survived King Philip's War only to die of starvation because the fields were trampled or never got planted. The Massachusetts Bay Colony almost went bankrupt, and 12 towns vanished.

Massasoit was a friend of the English colonists. The first New England settlers might not have survived without his help, and they knew it. Once, when he seemed near death, a group of settlers came from Plymouth with goose soup and a broth made from the root of the sassafras tree. Massasoit got better.

Massasoit's people, the Wampanoags, were hunters and fishermen and farmers whose lives turned with the cycle of the seasons. They were peaceful people and good neighbors. When some Pilgrims visited his village, Massasoit honored them by letting them spend the night on a plank bed with himself, his wife, and two of his chiefs.

A year after the Pilgrims arrived, Massasoit signed a treaty of peace with them. For more than 50 years, while he lived, there was peace in Massachusetts. But, even before he died, there were some—Indians and English—who saw trouble ahead. Mostly it was because there were so many English men and women. At first there had been only a few of these newcomers, but soon they were pushing the natives off the land.

Massasoit's two sons were troubled. Their generation was different from that of their father. They were not awed by the English, as their father sometimes seemed. The two boys were Wamsutta and Metacom, but Massasoit had asked the General Court in Plymouth to give them English names. So they were named for ancient kings of Greece: Alexander and Philip.

When his father died, Wamsutta-Alexander became ruler. Some Englishmen feared him. They sent troops, dragged him to Plymouth, threatened him, and acted haughty and superior.

As the Indians' land shrank, King Philip *(above)* told a friend, "I am resolved not to see the day when I have no country."

Alexander became ill and died on his way home. Metacom-Philip was now leader of his people. He believed the English had killed his brother, and he wanted revenge.

Besides, Metacom saw that the new people were destroying his land. (The English now called him King Philip. Some meant it respectfully, but others were mocking when they used the title.) And so Metacom began visiting other Indian leaders trying to convince them to join him to fight the English and drive them from America. That wasn't easy. There was no history of Indian unity. The Indian peoples were as different from each other as Swedes are from Spaniards, or Chinese from Pakistanis. They were descended from different peoples who came in different waves of immigration over the Bering Strait.

Metacom wasn't ready when war began. As with many wars, it was really an accident that started things. A Christian Indian named John Sassamon was killed. Sassamon had been to Harvard and was a friend of the Plymouth colonists. Today, no one is sure who killed him, but the English executed three members of Metacom's tribe for the murder. Metacom was furious. He attacked for revenge.

King Philip's War had begun. It was fought, off and on, for two years, 1675 and 1676, and it was horrible. If you have read about Indian wars—with scalpings, torched villages, tomahawks, and war whoops—you may have been reading about this war. Both sides were incredibly brutal.

Six hundred colonists lost their lives in King Philip's War; 3,000 Indians lost theirs. Fifty of ninety English villages were attacked; many were burned to the ground. The peaceful Narraganset Indians, who had nothing to do with the war, were massacred on their own land in Rhode Island because some of the settlers now feared all Indians. Many

The Pequot War

The Pequots were Indians who lived in New England near Narragansett Bay. Settlers moved into their territory until the Pequots controlled less and less of it. The Indians got angry about this, and killed some settlers and traders. In 1636, the colonists retaliated (fought back) by destroying a Pequot village. The next year war broke out. Captain John Mason (who founded New Hampshire), and his allies from the Mohican and Narraganset tribes, attacked the Pequots' fort, near what is now West Mystic, Connecticut. The Indians inside were burned alive. Those who didn't die were sold into slavery. The Pequots were almost wiped out. It was a taste of what was to come in King Philip's War.

Colonists confront Indians during King Philip's War. Bows and arrows were faster, but guns seemed scary and noisy.

innocent white people were killed in Indian raids of revenge.

Indian disunity hurt their cause. Some tribes helped the English. In addition, Indian warriors weren't used to long wars. They knew how to attack and destroy in quick raids. When the war went on and on, many Indians got tired of it. They wanted to plant their crops and get back to normal activities. They deserted their leader. Finally Metacom was trapped in a swamp, where he was killed by an Indian who was loyal to the colonists. Metacom's head was chopped off and hung on the fort at Plymouth; there it stayed for 25 years. His wife, children, and other captured Indians were sold in the West Indies as slaves.

It was a pattern that was repeated over and over again until the Indians could fight no more.

Tomahawk comes from an Algonquian word for a war club, *tamahakan*.

This skeleton was found in a shallow grave in South Glastonbury, Connecticut. It is thought to be the remains of a Narraganset Indian shot in King Philip's War. A doctor who examined the skeleton in 1959 said that the man was a runner. He died of peritonitis, which developed as a result of his wound.

23 The Indians Win This One

The Spaniards felt it was their duty to convert Indians to Christianity. Their missions did double duty as military forts.

The Spanish missions were small farms built around a church. Sometimes soldiers lived nearby in forts called "presidios." Sometimes the mission and the presidio were combined. Indians lived in the missions and did most of the farming and building. The priests taught them to read and write and to become Christians.

A priest, Fray Marcos de Niza, and a black man named Estebán were the first Old World explorers in New Mexico. They were looking for gold and the seven cities of Cíbola. They didn't find either.

At the very time that Metacom was fighting to free his land from the English invaders, an Indian leader, a man named Popé (poe-PAY) was preparing for the same kind of fight. Popé lived far away, thousands of miles across the continent, in a place the Spaniards called New Mexico. He was a religious leader and a great medicine man, and he would win his battle. He would drive the enemy from his country.

It is 1676 and revolution is brewing in the valley of the river that the Indians call "Big River." The white men call it "Rio Grande" (that means "big river" in Spanish).

The people of the pueblos have seen their land invaded by Spanish men and women. Their people have died mysteriously from diseases that were never known before. The Spaniards are few, but their guns and horses give them power. The Indians are forced to grow crops for the Spaniards, to pay them taxes, to clean their houses, to do their heavy work. The Spaniards take much of their land and some of their women. The pueblo people are made to worship the Spanish god. The Indians believe there is truth in all religions, so they don't mind following the ways of the Catholic Church. But the Spanish priests say that only their religion is true. They call the Indian religion evil. They say that religious freedom is the freedom to worship false gods. The Spanish priests are determined to destroy the old Indian ways. Indian dances are forbidden, the masks of the Indian priests are burned, and so are their sacred kachina dolls, important in religious ceremonies. The priests report proudly to their bishops in Spain that they have destroyed 1,600 Indian masks.

The Pueblo people pretend to do as the Spaniards wish, but, secretly, they keep to the old ways. They train their medicine men in kivas, dark rooms with hidden entries that are dug deep in the ground. Popé is one of those who is trained to be a leader.

The Spaniards have spies among the Indians. They learn of the medicine men and they are enraged. Spanish soldiers round up 47 Indian religious leaders. Four are accused of witchcraft and are hanged in the big plaza in the town called Santa Fe. The others are whipped and thrown in a dungeon.

Now the Indians are furious; even those who have converted to Christianity are enraged. Great numbers of Native Americans march to Santa Fe. (The Indians know the town as "Bead Water.") The Spaniards have killed beloved Indian leaders; they have humiliated others. The most beloved of them all is the man named Popé.

His name means "ripe squash" in the Tewa language. We know little of him except that he was wise and good, and that he inspired others.

The Indians in Santa Fe say they will leave the valley forever if the men are not released. If the Indians leave, the Spaniards will have no one to work for them and they will starve. The Spaniards open the dungeon and let Popé and all the medicine men go.

Popé has learned that the Indians have power when they unite. He must unite his people. But that will not be easy. The pueblo people of the valley speak seven different languages.

Still, he does it. Popé talks to leaders in all the pueblos. He even meets with his people's ancient enemy, the Apache. The Apaches are not pueblo people; they are nomads who have come from the Great Plains. The Apaches agree to help. Plans are made with great secrecy, for the Spaniards have spies everywhere.

In August 1680 Popé is ready. He knows the Spaniards have heard of the plans; he knows they are suspicious; he decides to mislead them. So he sends runners with a message—a message in a knotted rope. The Spaniards capture the runners and the Spanish governor forces an Indian to read the message of the knots. There are four knots and it means the revolution will come in four days.

That's what the message says, and that is what Popé wants the Spaniards to believe. But the next day, before they have time to prepare, all up and down the valley, at every Spanish settlement, at exactly the same time, Indians attack—burning, killing, and destroying. By nightfall only two Spanish communities are left: Santa Fe and Isleta.

Both of those towns are put under siege. That means that if any-

The New Mexican colony got its start in 1598 when Juan de Oñate arrived from Mexico. Oñate, a Spaniard, married a woman whose grandfather was Hernando Cortés and whose great-grandfather was the Aztec emperor Moctezuma. In 1610 the settlement is moved to Santa Fe. What is going on in Plymouth in 1610? How about at Jamestown? St. Augustine?

Though thousands of Pueblo Indians converted to Christianity, most still held on to their own beliefs and ceremonies, such as the Green Corn Dance shown here.

Nomads are people who move a lot. They settle for a while in one place, grazing their flocks. When the land is used up, or the weather changes, they move on to another spot.

Franciscans preach the gospel to two Indian leaders and their wives. One priest was asked how many "true believers" there were among his Pueblo parishioners; he said, "I don't think I have any."

one comes out, the Indians will overwhelm him. Because the plans have been made so well, there is no one to come to the Spaniards' rescue. The Indians have destroyed the other Spanish towns. Popé knows no help will come from Mexico. It usually takes a year and a half for wagons to make that trip. Besides, the winter's heavy rains have flooded the Rio Grande. A wagon train with supplies is stuck in the mud on the wrong side of the river.

Popé gives the Spanish governor a choice: he can stay in Santa Fe and starve, or he can leave the land and take his people with him.

The Spaniards leave—all of them. They march away, back to Mexico. The Indians watch peacefully and let them go. Then they burn the Spanish churches, tear down the Spanish towns, and go back to their old ways. They have won their revolution against tyranny and unfair taxes and religious persecution.

But the leaders in Spain and Mexico don't give up easily. They will return to New Mexico. It will take 12 years, and Popé will be dead, but they will be back. They will deal with the natives again. The Spaniards and the Pueblo Indians will do the same things that Englishmen and East Coast Indians are doing: they will fight, steal, trade, make peace, and misunderstand each other. These are civilizations in conflict. If there is a way for them to live in harmony, no one seems wise enough to have found it.

In 1692 the colonial Spanish leader Don Diego de Vargas *(above)* **and about 100 men reenter Santa Fe without bloodshed. This peace does not last. A year later, a fierce battle is fought for the city. The Pueblos are no longer united, and Vargas wins. The Spaniards call it** *la Reconquista—* **the "reconquest."**

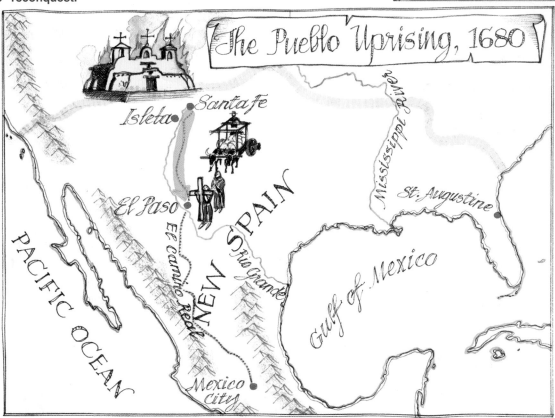

The Pueblo Uprising, 1680

24 What's a Colony?

The Indian on the seal of the Massachusetts Bay Colony is saying "Come over and help us"— which the Indians must have found hard to believe.

You may already know that England had 13 American colonies. I'll list them in just a minute.

First, do you remember what a colony is?

A colony is a place that belongs to another country. Think about a landlord and a renter. England, France, Spain, Holland, Sweden, and Portugal were all landlords in parts of America. They thought they owned the place. Then their colonists, the renters, said, "We're tired of belonging to someone else. We intend to own our own land." When that happened there were revolutions, and the landlords were forced to pack up and go home.

The east coast of North America was an English colony from 1607, when Jamestown began, until the Declaration of Independence was signed in 1776. Those were colonial times.

It was a long time. 1776 minus 1607 is...you can do the arithmetic yourself. When it comes to families, it was about seven generations. That means from son to father to grandfather to great-grandfather to great-great-

Massachusetts minted Pine Tree shillings (above). The $40 bill was backed by Spanish silver.

An artist who lived in the 19th century made this somewhat prettified portrait of an early colonial kitchen. A real 17th-century kitchen was probably barer and dirtier than this, with less furniture and fewer utensils and pots.

grandfather to great-great-great-grandfather to—whew—great-four-times-grandfather. A lot of things can happen in seven generations.

So when you read about colonial times, don't be surprised if you read different descriptions.

When the first colonists arrived, there were no friends to greet them. No houses were ready for them. They had to start from scratch—and I do mean scratch, as in scratching. The early colonists often had to live in huts of branches and dirt, or Indian wigwams, or even caves, and none of those places was bug-proof. And, of course, they had to scratch a living out of the ground.

Later colonists lived in small wooden houses with one or two rooms. Eventually, some lived in fine houses. A few lived in mansions, with beautiful furniture and paintings and dishes and silver. But no one had a bathroom like you have, or electric lights, or a furnace, or running water, or kitchen appliances. And very few people lived in mansions anyway.

You'll be reading about all 13 of the English colonies, because

In 1633, the Dutch brought a schoolmaster to the city of New Amsterdam to teach their children. He was Adam Roelantsen (ROY-lant-sun), and he founded the first school in the North American colonies. Today that school is the Collegiate School in New York City. Two years later, in 1635, Boston Latin School was opened. It was the first public school in the colonies. It, too, still exists.

ENGLISH
COLONIES
About 1740

MAINE
Part of
Massachusetts

New
Hampshire

CLAIMED BY N.H. and N.Y.

New
York

Mass

IROQUOIS Connecticut Rhode
Island

Pennsylvania

New
Jersey

Delaware

DELAWARE
INDIANS

Maryland

Appalachian Mountains

SHAWNEE Virginia

North
Carolina

CHEROKEE

South
Carolina

Georgia
CREEK

N

ATLANTIC
OCEAN

they turned into the United States. To get started, we need some organization. We're going to divide the colonies into three groups: north, south, and middle.

Look at the map and you'll see the New England colonies, the Middle Atlantic colonies, and the Southern colonies.

You know a whole lot about New England, so here's a test. Name the New England colonies. (Without checking on the page opposite.)

Did you get them all?

Did you goof and say Maine? Remember, Maine was not a separate colony; it was part of Massachusetts. We haven't said anything about Vermont. Today Vermont is a New England state, and a beautiful one, but it was not a separate colony.

(Remember, don't confuse states with colonies. The 13 colonies will turn into states when the Constitution is written and our nation—the United States—is formed.)

You already know about one Southern colony, Virginia. You will learn about Maryland, North Carolina, South Carolina, and Georgia. (Some people call Maryland a middle colony, but I don't.)

Coming next in this book are the Middle Colonies: New York, New Jersey, Delaware, and Pennsylvania.

First up is New York, where the Dutch are in control. It's hard for us to realize now that tiny Holland was once a great power. The Dutch had colonies all over the world. A business firm, the Dutch West India Company, owned most of the colonies, just as the Virginia and Plymouth companies owned English colonies.

Jonas Michaelius (mick-AY-lee-uss)

Sheep were very important before the colonies grew much cotton. Sheep grow heavy coats in winter, so their wool is sheared in spring.

came to New York in 1628. It was called New Netherland then, and the Dutch West India Company was in charge. That company had promised Michaelius a home in the New World. Here is part of a letter Michaelius wrote soon after he arrived:

The promise which the Lords Masters of the Company had made me to make myself a home…is wholly of no avail. For their honors well know that there are no horses, cows, or laborers to be obtained here for money….The country yields many good things for the support of life, but they are all to be gathered in an uncultivated and wild state.

The Dutch West India Company made promises that couldn't be kept. The Virginia Company did the same thing at Jamestown. (Those early Virginia settlers really expected to find gold on the ground.)

The Puritans always told the truth about their colony. So did a man named William Penn who owned a colony. (Yes, some individuals did own colonies.) We'll get to William Penn and his colony when we finish with New Netherland.

That small Dutch colony was just a trading post. The Dutch thought India—with its silks and spices—was much more important than America. But, just in case America did turn out to be valuable, they decided to do some fur trading on this continent.

The New England colonies are: Massachusetts, New Hampshire, Rhode Island, and Connecticut.

Henry Hudson: New York's Explorer

Henry Hudson knew he had found something special on a September day in 1609 when he sailed his small Dutch ship, the *Half Moon*, into the river that would bear his name. He was looking for the Northwest Passage, and the river seemed likely. It was deep and full of salmon, mullet, and other fish.

The *Half Moon* sailed jauntily, a carved red lion with a golden mane jutting out from its forward tip. The lion was splendid, and so was the whole ship. The bow (the front part of the boat) was bright green, with carved sailors' heads in shades of red and yellow. The decks—the forecastle and the poop—were painted pale blue with white clouds. The stern (the rear of the ship) was royal blue, with stars and a picture of the Man in the Moon. That wasn't all: there were glowing lanterns and flags—the Dutch flag, the flags of all seven Dutch provinces, the flag of the Dutch East India Company, and more.

Now, what would you have thought if you were a Native American standing on the shore of Manhattan Island, and this great colorful seabird appeared with men standing on its back? Remember, this was 1609, and the *Half Moon* was probably the first European ship you'd ever seen. At first the Indians thought it had come from God, and that the men aboard were his messengers. It wasn't long, however, before they realized they were just men.

25 Silvernails and Big Tub

The Dutch had good relations with the Indians. One of their treaties said they would "keep the Great Chain of Friendship polished bright."

New Amsterdam's coat of arms was flanked by a pair of beavers—and fur trading paid the bills.

Slave Market

In 1709, a market was set up on the corner of Wall and Water streets. It was a slave market: a place where men, women, and children were bought and sold. New York paved its streets with money raised by a tax on each slave brought into its port. By the middle of the 18th century, one in every ten New Yorkers was black. Most of them were slaves, but some were free; a few owned indentured white servants—"bound" men, women, girls, and boys.

"Old Silvernails" is what they called him, because the stick of wood that stood in place of his right leg was decorated with silver nails. He had lost the leg in a battle in the West Indies. His real name was Peter Stuyvesant (STY-viss-unt), and he was a Dutch governor and a hard-swearing, tough man. Maybe the Dutch thought Silvernails Stuyvesant was the right kind of person to run a colony in America. Maybe they didn't have any other volunteers. When it came to colonial leaders, the Dutch came up with some strange men.

They had a great piece of property, but they didn't seem to realize that. They just kind of fooled around on the North American continent. They were more serious in other parts of the globe.

Back in 1609, Henry Hudson, an Englishman sailing for the Netherlands, had gone up the river that is now called the Hudson. Because of that voyage, Holland claimed a large hunk of American land. It was land wedged between the stern Puritans in the North and the Anglican tobacco planters in the South; the Dutch called it New Netherland. (Today we know it as New York and New Jersey.)

In case you're confused: Holland, the Netherlands, and the land of the Dutch are all the same place. Why don't you find it on a map? And, while you're looking, can you find England? Can you see why both nations became sea powers? Now, cross the Atlan-

Peter Stuyvesant is still remembered in New York, where a high school is named after him.

Three early views of New Amsterdam. The big picture shows the town as seen from the village of Breukelen (today's Brooklyn Heights) across the East River. The plan at right looks down, showing the line of the city wall. The third picture shows the view from across the Hudson River, in New Jersey. In the 17th century, most of Manhattan was farmland.

tic. Put a finger on New York Harbor. Go up the Hudson River and look for a passage to China. You'll be stopped by rapids in the river when you get to Albany. That's what happened to Henry Hudson.

In 1626 the Dutch West India Company made what may be the most famous real-estate deal in history. It bought Manhattan Island (now the center of New York City) and Long Island from the Indians who lived there for some beads and goods said to be worth $24. Since the Indians didn't think people could own land, they may have thought they were outsmarting the white men.

By this time, the Dutch had decided that American furs might be almost as good as American gold, so they set up some trading posts. People in Europe were eager to buy American furs. Beaver, bear, fox, and other fur pelts could be made into sumptuous hats, coats, and blankets. The Dutch merchants hoped to get rich in the New World.

On Manhattan Island the people from Holland built a town called New Amsterdam. At one end they put a wall because they feared wolves and because cities in Europe had walls. Today that wall is the site of a famous street. Can you guess what it is called? Outside the wall were farms, which the Dutch called *bouweries*. Today a street

You guessed it—Wall Street!

97

Settlers in New Sweden trading with Delaware Indians. In 1643 the Swedes sold arms to the Delaware, who were fighting a Maryland tribe. Here they are making a deal to use the Indians' land for trapping furs.

Manhattan is an island 12½ miles from end to end. Broadway, its longest street, runs the length of the island.

in New York is called "the Bowery." (It doesn't look much like a farm now.)

Because of its great harbor, New Amsterdam was soon a sailor's town, bustling with people who arrived on ships from faraway places. It was said that you could hear 18 different languages being spoken in the city of New Amsterdam. Right away, in 1626, the Dutch brought slaves to New Amsterdam. You could buy a slave for about the same amount it would cost to pay a worker one year's salary. So some people thought it made good sense to own slaves. It was an economic, or money, decision.

One day a ship sailed into New Amsterdam's harbor with a group of Jews aboard. Peter Stuyvesant didn't want them to land. He was a bigot and didn't believe in religious freedom. Stuyvesant was a member of the Dutch Reformed Church and saw no reason to tolerate others. "Giving them liberty," he wrote ("them" meant the Jews), "we cannot refuse the Lutherans and Papists [Catholics]." But the Dutch West India Company said the Jews could stay, so there was nothing Stuyvesant could do.

Grouchy Old Silvernails was in charge of all of New Netherland. He was pretty good at running things, but he would stomp his wooden leg and swear at anyone who disagreed with him. When the Dutchmen who had been elected councilors objected to something he said, he called them "ignorant subjects." Another time he said he would ship them back to Holland—in pieces—if they gave him trouble.

But if you were going to run a swearing contest, Stuyvesant might lose. Johan Printz (YO-han PRINCE) had a mouth that was even more foul. He was governor of New Sweden, on the Delaware Bay, not far from New Netherland.

Printz was a whale of a man. The Indians called him Big Tub, and he may have been the biggest man on the continent. He was seven feet tall and weighed 400 pounds. Big Tub was an autocrat—an absolute ruler—and he liked to hang people who opposed him. But he did hold his colony together for 10 years, with very little help from the Swedes at home. And he introduced a new style of architecture, the log cabin, that became popular in frontier settlements.

Finally, Johan Printz got tired of trying to run things himself and went back to Sweden. The new Swedish governor decided to get tough and capture a Dutch fort, but he didn't realize what Old Silvernails was like. Stuyvesant sent seven ships, and that wiped out the Swedish colony.

That made Stuyvesant popular in New Amsterdam—but not for long. Nine years later, in 1664, the English decided to do to the Dutch what the Dutch had done to the Swedes. Old Silvernails stomped on his wooden leg, but nobody came to his rescue. The British took New Amsterdam without firing a shot. They renamed it New York.

The Hon. Peter Stuyvesant

a Pennsylvania Bank Barn

Wooden Rocking Horse

Printing Press

Ice Skates

Small Windmill

Indian corn

Alcove Bed

Crabs and Tavern signs.

The MIDDLE COLONIES

St. Lawrence R.

Lake Ontario

CLAIMED BY N.H.

Hudson R.

Albany

NEW YORK

PENNSYLVANIA

Susquehanna R.

Delaware R.

New York

Long Island

NEW JERSEY

Lancaster

Philadelphia

Atlantic Ocean

N W E S

DELAWARE

1794

J. VAN DER HAYDEN

ENTERTAINMENT

26 West to Jersey

James, Duke of York, later became James II, king of England, but he was not popular.

The English came up with the name Holland, meaning "hollow land." They were thinking of the center of the country, which is unusually flat. Much of Holland's land was once under water. Beginning in the 12th century, the Dutch built dikes, which are sea walls. Then they drained the land. The dikes kept the ocean from returning. Do you know the story of the boy who put his finger in a hole in a dike and saved his people from drowning? That famous fictional tale comes from *Hans Brinker and the Silver Skates,* written by Mary Mapes Dodge, an American woman who never went to Holland!

The Netherlands pulled down its flag and left America. It was 1664, and the Dutch had been here for 50 years. During those years they had gone up the Hudson River, built a town at Fort Orange (Albany), and established big plantations along the river. The Dutch farm owners were called "patroons." People came from Holland to work the patroons' farms. They brought their tulips, their hardworking habits, their neatness, and their storytelling ways with them. (Their children's favorite story was about a fellow named Santa Claus, who visited just before Christmas, on December 6.)

Actually, most of the Dutch people didn't leave, and the British even let Peter Stuyvesant stay. They let the Dutch have religious freedom. The Netherlanders just weren't in charge anymore. It was the Duke of York who owned the place now.

The Duke of York was named James, and his brother was the king of England. York (that is what some people called James) was one of the owners of the Royal African Company, which controlled the British slave trade. It seems to have occurred to the duke that if he encouraged the use of slaves in the New World, he would make lots of money. And that is just what happened.

York must have been conceited and vain, because you can see what he named his land. Well, that isn't quite true. It wasn't all called New York. Some of it became New Jersey. The Duke of York gave a big chunk of land to two of his friends. One of them, Sir George Carteret, came from the island of Jersey, which explains why it was "New" Jersey. The duke's other friend was Lord John Berkeley. Berkeley's brother was governor of Virginia.

Those two owners were called "proprietors." They expected the people who lived on their land to pay them a tax called a "quit rent." That didn't make them very popular.

But they had good qualities all the same. They wrote a plan of government, a charter, that was the best any English colony had. It set up an assembly that represented the settlers. (Assemblies, parliaments, and congresses are all similar organizations.) The charter provided for freedom of religion. You could be a Quaker or a Puritan or an Anglican in New Jersey, and, as long as you were a man, you had the right to vote. You didn't have that freedom in Massachusetts or Virginia or most of the other colonies.

Soon people were pouring into New Jersey from all over: Finns, Swedes, Germans, English and others. In New Jersey everybody lived together in harmony.

At first New Jersey was divided into East Jersey and West Jersey. Then the king bought out the proprietors, united New Jersey, and made it a royal colony. That meant the king was now the owner of New Jersey. He sent a royal governor to take charge and collect his rents. The king allowed the colonists to keep making their own laws through the elected assembly.

For a while, New Jersey was part of the western frontier of the country. The frontier was land that was on the edge of what Europeans considered civilization. If you look at a map, you can see where the frontier of European civilization was in 1700. Is there a frontier today? Where might it be? Clue: look up.

Fort Orange, which became Albany, was established as a fur trading post before New Amsterdam.

These are rows of old Dutch houses in Albany.

27 Cromwell and Charles

Charles didn't have to lose his head, but he wouldn't give his opponents an inch. That was his downfall.

Even though this is a book about US, you need to keep up with events in England, because what was going on there was very important to the colonists in America. And something unexpected was happening in England. A civil war was being fought. The war was between King Charles I and the Puritans. The king lost the war. Then the Puritans executed him. (Kings are never killed, they are executed.)

Are you surprised about the civil war? Are you surprised that the English would chop off their king's head? Back then a lot of people were astonished.

Some people called the new government the "Protectorate." Some people called it the pits.

Virginians were on the side of the king; people on that side were called "Cavaliers." (They got that name because the king's soldiers fought mostly on horseback, and soldiers on horseback are called "cavalry.")

The New Englanders, naturally, were for the Puritans, who were sometimes called "Round-heads." (They wore their hair short at a time when many men wore their hair long.) When they needed a haircut, Puritan men would put a bowl on their heads and cut around the bowl, as in the picture in chapter 21.)

Put 1649 in your head. Because—talking about heads—1649 was the year Charles I lost his. It was an important moment in history because

Oliver Cromwell *(right)* was a very good general who often beat the Royalists even when he was outnumbered. He wasn't a very good ruler, unfortunately.

it reminded people that kings could be overthrown. And, though it happened in England, it helped bring freedom to Americans.

That revolution in 1649—and it really was a revolution—was called the English Civil War. I'll say it again, because it is so important: in 1649 the Puritans won the English Civil War, and Charles I lost his head. Some people think this revolution was a failure—because, as you will soon learn, kings came back. But it wasn't a failure. The Civil War made an important point: people can change their government if they want to badly enough.

But now we're in 1649, and, since poor King Charles I is without a head, the Puritan leader, Oliver Cromwell, takes charge of the government. I would like to tell you that Cromwell does a splendid

At King Charles's trial, the judge put on a scarlet gown to read the death sentence: "Charles Stuart is a tyrant, traitor, murderer, and public enemy to the good people of this nation, and shall be put to death by the severing of his head from his body."

The first Cavaliers are swaggering young men who act as Charles's personal guard.

The Plague that devastates London in Charles II's reign ends with another disaster—the Great Fire of 1666. The fire starts in a bakery and spreads quickly. Soon most of London's old wooden houses are gone. So are the Plague germs.

job as ruler, but he doesn't. When the Puritans take power they destroy many Anglican churches, break church windows, smash statues, and burn great works of art. They even kill some Catholics and Anglicans, just because of their religion.

Oliver Cromwell tries to do what he thinks is right. He is a strong leader, and he does do many good things. But he doesn't understand that his opponents have rights, too. You could call him a tyrant and not be wrong.

One of the first things the Puritans do is to close all the theaters in London. That is going too far. London is known for its theaters and its free-speaking plays. A few of the plays in London are wicked and others mock politicians. Tyrants (wherever they are) never appreciate free speech. (Why?)

Besides, the Puritans don't have much of a sense of humor. In one of Shakespeare's plays, called *Twelfth Night,* Sir Toby Belch, a clown-like character, makes fun of Puritan behavior. Sir Toby says, "Dost thou think, because thou art virtuous, there shall be no more cakes and ale?" (What does he mean by that?) The Puritans won't even let Shakespeare's plays be seen. (Shakespeare died in 1616.)

When Cromwell dies (in 1658), his son Richard—who is known as "Tumbledown Dick"—tries to take over. Dick is a quiet man who likes farming and sports better than ruling. He can't hold on to power. Besides, the English people are tired of the stern Puritans, and they want to have fun. They want cakes and ale. So they put the old king's son on the throne. He is Charles II, and because of his good nature he is known as the "merry monarch." The time in which he rules is called the "Restoration." (You can see why it is the Restoration—kings were *restored* to power.)

But Charles isn't so merry when it comes to the Puritans. He kills some of them, and he digs up Cromwell's body and cuts off his head. Now Puritans are being mistreated. Things get so bad during the Restoration that many Puritans leave England and come to America.

Some of the king's friends come, too. When Charles II becomes king, he decides to reward friends who stayed loyal to his family while Cromwell was running things. He gives them gifts of America. As you know, he gives his brother, the Duke of York, the gift of New Netherland. (Then he sends an army to take it from the Dutch.)

He gives the Carolinas to eight of his favorite lords. He gives Pennsylvania to a young man whose religion makes it dangerous for him to live in England. In the next chapter I will tell you why.

28 William the Wise

"I have led the greatest colony into America that ever any man did upon a private credit."

William Penn was born with a silver spoon in his mouth and servants at his feet. His father was an important admiral: rich, Anglican, and a friend of King Charles II.

What did William Penn do when he grew up? He became a member of a radical, hated, outcast sect, the Society of Friends, also known as the Quakers.

What did being a Quaker do for William Penn? It got him kicked out of college when he refused to attend Anglican prayers. It got him a beating from his father, who wanted him to belong to the Church of England. It led him to jail for his beliefs—more than once. It gave him a faith that he carried through his life. And it also gave him a reason for founding an American colony.

King Charles II liked William Penn in spite of his religion. Everyone, it seems, was charmed by his sweet ways. But when Penn came before the king and refused to take off his hat—Quakers defer only to God—some people gasped and wondered if Penn's head, along with his hat, might be removed. But Charles, the "merry monarch," must have been in a good mood. As the story goes, he laughed and doffed his own hat, saying, "Only one head can be covered in the presence of a king."

Now King Charles had borrowed money from Admiral Penn, and a goodly sum it must have been, because, after the admiral died, when William asked that the debt be paid with land in America, he was given a tract of land larger than all of England. King Charles named it Pennsylvania, which means "Penn's woods."

Pennsylvania was situated midway between the pious Puritans in

You've probably noticed that the spelling of the documents quoted in this book isn't always the same as the spelling you've learned. Until Noah Webster wrote a speller (in 1783) and an American dictionary (in 1828), there was no standard spelling. People just wrote words the way that seemed right to them. Sometimes the same word could be spelled two different ways in a single sentence.

An Historical and Geographical Account
OF THE
PROVINCE and COUNTRY
OF
PENSILVANIA;
AND OF
West-New-Jersey
IN
AMERICA.

The Richness of the Soil, the Sweetness of the Situation, the Wholesomness of the Air, the Navigable Rivers, and others, the prodigious Encrease of Corn, the flourishing Condition of the City of *Philadelphia*, with the stately Buildings, and other Improvements there. The strange Creatures, as Birds, Beasts, Fishes, and Fowls, with the several sorts of Minerals, Purging Waters, and Stones, lately discovered The Natives, Aborigines, their Language, Religion, Laws, and Customs; The first Planters, the Dutch, Sweeds, and English, with the number of its Inhabitants; As also a Touch upon George Keith's New Religion, in his second Change since he left the QUAKERS

With a Map of both Countries.

By GABRIEL THOMAS,
who resided there about Fifteen Years.

London, Printed for, and Sold by *A. Baldwin*, at the Oxon Arms in *Warwick-Lane*, 1698.

Gabriel Thomas, one of the earliest settlers in Pennsylvania, wrote a pamphlet in praise of its charms—you can read his words on page 108.

Charles II died a Catholic at heart, but he admired William Penn enough to let him practice his religion in America.

Your *conscience* is your sense of right and wrong. It's something that tells you when you're doing right and warns you when you're doing wrong. *Conscientious* means being careful to do what you know is right.

New England and the convivial Anglicans in the South. Quakers weren't wanted in either region.

Thanks to William Penn, Quakers now had their own colony. But he made it different from most of the other colonies. Penn really believed in brotherly love. He said that Pennsylvania was not just for Quakers but for everyone.

The king had picked a good man to lead a colony—perhaps the best of all who tried it. Penn was an educated man, a philosopher, a town planner, and a lawyer. He wanted Pennsylvania to be a colony where Quaker ideas about peace and goodness would prevail.

In England, Quakers seemed a threat to everyone who felt comfortable with the old, established ways of thinking. The country had beheaded a king, and that didn't work out. New ideas seemed dangerous, as they often do. Quakers had notions that would change Old England. Wealthy citizens didn't want things to change, so it was poor people, mostly, who were Quakers.

In Penn's day, some people—ministers, kings, lords, and dukes—were considered superior to the average person. They expected others to bow to them, but Quakers wouldn't. They wouldn't bow to anyone. They even refused to pay taxes to support the Church of England. Can you see a problem? The Anglicans did.

England had lords and ladies in the rich upper class, merchants and farmers in the middle class, and peasants and poor people in the lower class. It was almost impossible to rise from the lower class to the upper. The upper-class lords and earls often acted as if they were better than anyone else. It was that class system that made many ambitious people come to the New World. In America, with hard work, many poor people would rise to the top.

Because the Bible says, "Thou shalt not kill," Quakers believe all war is wrong. They won't fight even when drafted into the army. They are called "conscientious objectors," because their conscience tells them not to fight.

And they won't swear allegiance to a king or government or flag or anyone but God. That was another real problem in England, where people were expected to swear their loyalty to the king.

William Penn wanted to practice Quaker ideas in America. That

The South East Prospect of The City of Philadelphia By Peter Cooper Painter

meant treating all people as equals and respecting all religions. Those new ideas of "toleration" and "natural rights" were confusing. It was difficult for good people to know what was right.

Do you understand the difference between toleration and equality? Some colonies offered freedom of religion but not equality. You could practice any religion but you couldn't vote or hold office (be a mayor or sheriff) unless you belonged to the majority's church. That wasn't true in Penn's colony. While he was in charge, all religions were equal.

When Penn said all people, he meant *all* people. Quakers were among the first to object to Negro slavery and, more than anyone else, to treat Indians as equals. In 1681, William Penn wrote a letter to the Native Americans of Pennsylvania. He said:

> may [we] always live together as neighbors and friends, else what would the great God say to us, who hath made us not to devour and destroy one another, but live soberly and kindly together in the world?

Penn proposed a "firm league of peace." He continued:

> I am very sensible of the unkindness and injustice that hath been too much exercised toward you by the people of these parts of the world…but I am not such a man…I desire to win and gain your love and friendship by a kind, just, and peaceable life.

Penn was generous as well as fair. He offered land on easy terms to those who came to his colony.

On his first visit to America, he sailed up the Delaware River and picked the site of Pennsylvania's first capital, Philadelphia. Then he helped plan the city by using a pattern of crossing streets, called a "grid," that would be copied throughout the new land. He gave numbers to all the streets that went in one direction; the streets that went the other way he gave tree names, like Pine and Chestnut and Walnut. Philadelphia is still thought of as a fine example of town planning.

Penn wrote a Charter of Liberties for Pennsylvania. Penn said the charter set up a government "free to the people under it, where the

This view of Philadelphia, painted by Peter Cooper in about 1720, is the oldest surviving canvas of any American city.

William Penn planned his city, Philadelphia, without walls or fortifications, because he expected its citizens to be peaceful.

Today the capital of Pennsylvania is Harrisburg.

107

laws rule, and the people are a party to those laws."

The southeastern part of Pennsylvania was called the "Three Lower Counties." In 1704 those counties asked for their own assembly and William Penn gave it to them. In 1776 they became an independent state named Delaware.

William Penn didn't stay in America for long. He had business to attend to in England, and so he chose rulers for Pennsylvania. Since he owned the place, he had a right to do that.

Penn did not believe in democracy. (Hardly anyone did at the beginning of the 18th century.) He was an aristocrat. In those days, ordinary people were not thought to be capable of picking their own leaders. William Penn thought he was choosing good people to lead his colony. But, as it turned out, he was too trusting.

The men he picked to run his colony fought among themselves and cheated him. (He would have been better off if he had believed in democracy.) William Penn lost most of his fortune developing Pennsylvania.

But Penn did prove that freedom and fairness work. Philadelphia was soon the largest, most prosperous city in the colonies. People came from Germany, France, Scotland, and Wales—as well as England—looking for religious freedom and a good place to live. One, a boy named Benjamin Franklin, came from Boston.

William Penn and the Indians make peace, in this painting by Edward Hicks.

29 Ben Franklin

Franklin was famous for his countrified appearance. The French couldn't get over his fur hat.

Some people had problems with Benjamin Franklin. They accused him of not having any gravity. Now that doesn't mean he floated around like a weightless space voyager. *Gravity* has another meaning, as in "grave." No, not a place where you get buried, but you are getting closer. Someone who is grave is very serious, maybe a bit dull, and certainly not much fun. Ben Franklin did have a problem. He just couldn't stay serious or dull. He was always playing jokes or having fun.

The French had no trouble with Ben. They loved his jokes and admired his good mind. They were amazed by all the things he had done. He was a scientist, an inventor, a writer, and a great patriotic American.

His mind never seemed to stop for rest. Daylight saving time was his idea; and he invented bifocal glasses, the lightning rod, the one-arm desk chair, and an efficient stove. He founded the first public library, the first city hospital, and the University of Pennsylvania. He was the most famous journalist of his time, and the first editor to use cartoons as illustrations. He made electricity into a science. And that is only part of what he did.

Benjamin Franklin helped with the ideas that made this country special, and he got the French to help pay for the revolution that made us free.

But, as I said, some people had problems with Franklin. The English people didn't much like him. Well, that's not quite true. It was English politicians who didn't like him, especially when the colonies began to object to the way England was treating them.

When Ben was sent to London to represent the Americans, one Englishman wrote, "I look upon him as a dangerous engine." And Lord

109

Poor Richard, 1733.
AN
Almanack
For the Year of Chrift
1733,
eing the F...ft after LEAP YEAR:

Just a few examples of Franklin's many interests. Clockwise from lower left: a Franklin stove, bifocals, a copy of Poor Richard's Almanack, *a two-faced clock (the lower part tells hours and minutes, the upper part tells seconds—but it was too hard to read and never caught on), and, of course, a printing press.*

Sandwich (that really was his name) called him one of the "most mischievous enemies" that England ever knew. (By the way, sandwiches were named for Lord Sandwich, whose real name was John Montagu. He liked his servants to fix him a snack—meat between bread—when he played cards.)

Some Americans accused Franklin of liking the English too much; the English, of course, said he didn't like them at all. What Ben was doing was trying to be fair and also trying to prevent war. He said, "There never was a good war or a bad peace."

I think you would have liked him. And if you want to have a real hero, someone to use as a guide for ordering your life, you can't do better than Benjamin Franklin. He had what has been called a "happy balance of earnestness and humor." He made the most of what he had.

One of his biographers wrote, "He had a talent for happiness." Another said, "He hated solemn pompous people....He gave away much of his money...he set about improving himself."

But you need to know something of his life, so you can judge the man yourself.

Benjamin Franklin was born in Boston, the 15th child in a family with 17 children. He was the youngest son of the youngest son of the youngest son—back to his great-great-grandfather. His father

Benjamin Franklin was born on January 17, 1706, and died on April 17, 1790. His life spanned the 18th century.

110

was a hardworking candlemaker descended from Puritan stock. Young Franklin went to school for three years, and then his parents could afford no more. It was enough to get him started; he loved books and reading, and he educated himself.

One thing he didn't like was candlemaking. So his father signed him as an apprentice to Ben's older half-brother, James, who was a printer. In return for room and board (food) and training, an apprentice had to work for a certain number of years. He was not free to quit. It was something like being an indentured servant. Ben was 12 years old, and his father signed him for nine years.

He didn't get along with his brother, and what he really wanted to do was to go to sea. But he made the best of a bad situation. The print shop was a good place to learn. There were stacks of books—he read them all—and interesting people dropped by. Some wrote for the newspaper James printed and owned.

Ben wanted to write for the paper, but he knew James wouldn't publish his work. So he wrote letters to the editor and signed them with the made-up name of a woman; he called her "Silence Dogood."

The letters were a big hit. Silence wrote that she was "naturally very jealous for the rights and liberties of my country: and the least appearance of an incroachment on those invaluable privileges, is apt to make my blood boil exceedingly."

When Dogood wrote a description of herself, it could have been a description of Franklin: "I never intend to wrap my talent in a napkin," she wrote. "To be brief; I am courteous and affable, good-humoured (unless I am first provoked), handsome, and sometimes witty."

Everyone wanted to know who Silence Dogood was. When Ben's brother found out, he stopped printing the letters.

Ben wasn't happy, but he didn't sit around and mope. One thing Benjamin Franklin did all his life was to try and find ways to improve himself. Maybe it was his Puritan background that made him industrious.

He decide he wanted to be a writer. Ben had learned to spell at

The earliest portrait of Ben Franklin in existence was painted in about 1748, when he was 42 years old and the postmaster of Philadelphia.

Incroachment (which we spell *encroachment*) means "taking another's possessions gradually or slyly." Usually the word is used to describe the illegal taking of land: "He encroached on his neighbor's property."

That's Franklin on the horse in the middle. He's being honored in a parade because he helped fight off Indian attacks on the Pennsylvania frontier in 1755.

Prose is plain language not arranged as verse.

Saucy means "fresh." A *shilling* was an English silver coin, worth one-twentieth of a pound.

the printing house, but his father told him that the style of his writing was not good. So he found a friend and they wrote letters back and forth. Then he worked out exercises to improve his writing style. Sometimes he turned stories into poems, then back again into prose. It was a fine way to learn to work with words.

When Ben was 16, he read about a vegetable diet. He became a vegetarian and bought books with the money he saved by not eating meat. Soon he could talk about books with anyone. He was becoming very well educated.

But he still had problems with his brother. "Perhaps I was too saucy and provoking," said Ben. "My brother was passionate, and had often beaten me, which I took extremely amiss." Finally, at 17, Ben ran away from Boston. He sold his books and used the money to get to Philadelphia. In his *Autobiography*, Franklin described his arrival in that city:

> *I was dirty from my journey; my pockets were stuffed out with shirts and stockings; I knew no soul nor where to look for lodging. I was fatigued with traveling, rowing, and want of rest; I was very hungry; and my whole stock of cash consisted of a Dutch dollar and about a shilling in copper. The latter I gave the people of the boat for my passage, who at first refused it on account of*

my rowing; but I insisted on their taking it, a man being some-
times more generous when he has but a little money than when he
has plenty, perhaps through fear of being thought to have but little.

Then I walked up the street, gazing about, till near the market
house I met a boy with bread. I had made many a meal on bread,
and inquiring where he got it, I went immediately to the baker's he
directed me to, in Second Street, and asked for biscuit, intending
such as we had in Boston; but they, it seems, were not made in
Philadelphia. Then I asked for a three-penny loaf, and was told they
had none such. So, not considering or knowing the difference of
money, and the greater cheapness nor the names of his bread, I bade
him give me three-penny-worth of any sort. He gave me, according-
ly three great puffy rolls. I was surprised at the quantity, but took
it, and, having no room in my pockets, walked off with a roll under
each arm, and eating the other. Thus I went up Market Street as
far as Fourth Street, passing by the door of Mr. Read, my future
wife's father; when she, standing at the door, saw me, and thought
I made, as I certainly did, a most awkward, ridiculous appearance.

That awkward boy soon had a job working for a printer. Then he got a chance to go to London. He went and had adventures and learned a lot. When he returned to Philadelphia, he opened a print shop. Soon he began publishing his own newspaper. He became the best printer in Philadelphia. Because he was so good, he printed all the official papers for the colony of Pennsylvania.

Then he decided to publish an almanac. In the 17th century, al-most every colonial home had two books: one was a Bible, the other was an almanac. The almanac was very useful. It had a calen-dar; it predicted the weather; it told when the moon would be full and when it would be a sliver; it told about the ocean's tides; and it was filled with odds and ends of information. Ben Franklin, with his curiosity, had a head filled with interesting information. His al-manac, called *Poor Richard's Almanack*, became very popular. Poor Richard was always giving advice. He said things like:

Early to bed and early to rise, makes a man healthy, wealthy and wise.
God helps them who help themselves.
Three may keep a secret, if two of them are dead.

The almanac made Benjamin Franklin rich. He decided to retire, at age 42, and spend the rest of his life doing all the things he want-ed to do. He studied electricity, invented things, became a politi-cian, and was soon Philadelphia's most famous citizen. He would help found a new nation. By his example he showed that in America a poor boy could become the equal of anyone in the world.

What did Ben Franklin say when he discovered electricity?

Nothing. He was too shocked.

If you would not be forgotten,
As soon as you are dead and rotten,
Either write things worth reading,
Or do things worth the writing.
—*Benjamin Franklin*

This was Benjamin Franklin's proposal for an experiment to decide whether lightning is electricity. "On the top of some high tower or steeple, place a kind of sentry-box...big enough to contain a man and an electric stand. From the middle of the stand let an iron rod rise and pass bending out of the door, and then upright 20 feet, pointed very sharp at the end. A man standing on it, when such clouds are passing low, might be electrified." He didn't un-derstand that being elec-trified can kill you.

30 Maryland's Form of Toleration

Cecil Calvert, Maryland's owner, could make his own coins —here's his face on a 1659 silver shilling.

Did you notice
that we have been traveling south? After New England we stopped in New York and New Jersey, and then Pennsylvania and Delaware. Now, if you look around, you'll see we've reached fertile, water-lapped Maryland.

Maryland is sometimes called a Southern colony and sometimes a Middle colony. During the Civil War it was a "Border colony." Can you guess why Maryland has had a hard time with its identity?

Sir George Calvert was an English lord and a real gentleman. That means he acted like one. He was not a poor boy who had to do everything for himself; he was wealthy, very wealthy. He was also energetic and daring.

Sir George made things hard for himself by becoming a Catholic. The English didn't like Catholics.

But, remember, the Spaniards, French, and Portuguese didn't like Protestants. This may seem a bit tiresome, but it was serious business back in the 17th century. You could get your head cut off if you practiced the wrong religion.

Sir George didn't get his head cut off, but he was forced to resign from his important government position. Since everyone liked him (he was a real gentleman), things worked out. The Irish—who were Catholic—were happy when the king gave him land in Ireland and named him Baron of Baltimore. Then King Charles I, who really liked Sir George, gave him a colony in America.

They named it Maryland. That was said to be in honor of the king's Catholic wife, Queen Henrietta Maria, although some say Calvert really meant to honor Mary, the mother of Jesus Christ.

Sir George dreamed of a colony "founded on religious freedom, where there would not only be a good life, but also a prosperous one, for those bold enough to take the risk." It was George Calvert's son, Cecil (SESS-ul), who actually founded the colony. He thought English Catholics could live in harmony there with Protestants.

Many Catholics did go to Maryland, but not as many as expected. Even Cecil, the new Lord Baltimore, didn't go. Cecil just stayed home and took the money that came from his colony.

The label on this 1638 map calls the area pictured "Nova Virginiae" (New Virginia). Today it's mostly Maryland, as you can tell by comparing the picture to a modern map. Look for the Susquehanna Indian woman (the map says "Sasquesahanoug") hunting with a bow and a club. At the upper left Powhatan holds court "as he did when Captain Smith was delivered to him prisoner." If you turn back to page 23, you'll see the map by John Smith that this map is based on. What had mapmakers learned about the area in the years since Smith's map?

He sent his younger brother, Leonard, to be the first governor. He told him to be "very careful to preserve unity and peace...and treat the Protestants with as much mildness and favor as justice will permit."

The Calverts ruled well. They saw that there was representative government and that people were treated fairly. In 1649, the Calverts urged the Maryland Assembly to pass a Toleration Act. The Assembly did—it was a landmark act. Religious freedom was a new

Baltimore *(below)* was a small but thriving township by the end of the 1700s.

At top left is George Calvert, who sought freedom for Catholics in Maryland. Below is Queen Henrietta Maria, the wife of King Charles I; at right, painted in 1761, is Calvert's great-great-great-great-great grandson, Charles—and, of course, a slave.

idea that was being talked about by European philosophers, and practiced by Quakers (who still seemed peculiar to most people). But now a conservative American colony was trying out that freedom with an official act.

The Calverts were being practical. They meant to protect the Catholic minority and encourage settlement. This first-step act allowed for freedom of religion—but *only for Christians.*

Anyone who did not believe in Christ was to be hanged. That meant Jews or atheists (people who don't believe there is a God), or even some Christians who asked too many questions. Those people had to keep quiet or leave Maryland.

It was also a hanging offense to curse God. If you made fun of Christian doctrine, the law said you were to be whipped in public.

That sounds harsh—and it was—but remember the times. In the colonies controlled by France, Spain, and Portugal no Protestants, Jews, or atheists were allowed at all.

Bound Out

A big problem for early colonists in America was the shortage of labor. There weren't enough people to farm and do all the other work. One way of dealing with this was slavery—and Maryland imported many slaves. Another was by bringing over servants and apprentices who were "bound out" to an employer for a certain number of years—four or five at least, and, if you were a boy or girl, often until you were 21. The employer fed, housed, and clothed you. In return, you had to work unpaid, usually learn-

ing a trade. If you had a good employer it probably wasn't a bad life; but if your employer was stingy or cruel, or just indifferent, it could be miserable. The newspapers were always full of wanted notices from employers whose bound men or apprentices had run away.

In Maryland, if you stuck the job out, the law said that when your term of service was up you were to be given 50 acres of land, a suit of clothes, an ax, two hoes, and three barrels of corn. Then, if you were a Christian white man, you could vote and be elected to the assembly.

A glassblower and his apprentice.

116

31 Carry Me Back to Ole Virginny

On this optimistic English tobacco label, colonists and an Indian chat happily together about the merits of the brand being advertised.

I haven't said much about Virginia since John Smith's time, and that's too bad, because some future presidents were getting born there: George Washington, Thomas Jefferson, James Madison, and James Monroe. Virginia's John Marshall, George Mason, and Patrick Henry were destined for greatness, too.

Was there something about Virginia that bred leaders? Life there was certainly different from life in Pennsylvania or Massachusetts.

Most people in 18th-century Virginia weren't Puritans or Quakers. They were Anglicans: members of the Church of England. But they were more relaxed about their religion than the Puritans. In the New England colonies the ministers were the most important people in the community; in the South, the wealthy landowners were more important.

The Virginians didn't live in towns, as people did in Massachusetts. They lived along the rivers on small farms, or on very large farms called "plantations." Living on the river made shipping easy, and that was important.

What Virginians were shipping was tobacco—to England. While a few other crops were grown, the

The slaves on a tobacco plantation don't just plant and pick and dry and cure the tobacco. The slaves do *all* the physical labor—here they're making the barrels to ship the tobacco, and packing them, too.

117

Splitting Shingles

Spinning Wool

Plantation Kitchen

Tobacco

Tobacco Barn

The SOUTHERN COLONIES

Baltimore

MARYLAND

Potomac R.

Williamsburg

James R.

Jamestown

VIRGINIA

Ohio R.

Appalachian Mountains

Roanoke R.

NORTH CAROLINA

SOUTH CAROLINA

Pee Dee R.

GEORGIA

Santee R.

Charleston

Savannah R.

Savannah

Altamaha R.

Atlantic Ocean

N
W   E
S

Canvasback Duck

Dress

Rice and Rice Hook

and Scales

Raccoon

main moneymaker was tobacco. That was a problem. When tobacco prices were high, Virginians did well. When tobacco prices fell, they were in trouble. There was no balance.

There was little industry, and most goods came from England. In this land of magnificent forests, even fine furniture and other wood products were shipped from the "mother country."

There was another problem. Tobacco uses up the soil. After a few years, nothing grows well on land that has been planted with tobacco. To succeed in a tobacco economy, you need to rest the land every few years. That means you need to own a lot of land. You also need many workers.

So tobacco growers in colonial Virginia began to buy land and workers. As you know, at first they bought indentured servants. Then they bought Africans and made them slaves. By 1750 there were more Africans in Virginia than any other single group of people. More Virginians had come from Africa than from England or Scotland.

It was a few rich white planters who held power in the colony. Most whites were small farmers, and there were thousands of them. Some owned a slave or two—or hoped to—and that made them go along with the big slave owners. Virginia was not the only place where this happened. A society built on slavery stretched from Maryland to Georgia. Slavery was not only terrible for the black slaves—it ruined many white farmers, too.

At first the South, like the North, was full of yeoman farmers. Yeomen are independent farmers who work their own land. When slave ships began bringing in large numbers of Africans, the yeomen were in trouble. The blacks, being slaves, were forced to work for nothing. The yeoman farmers couldn't compete with that. The tobacco they grew was more expensive than tobacco grown by slaves.

The yeoman farmers had these choices. They could stay in Virginia (or Maryland or the Carolinas or Georgia) and try to work their own farms. Usually that meant they would become "poor whites."

Or they could buy slaves.

Or they could head West, to the frontier, and settle new land (and perhaps fight Indians for that land). These were difficult choices.

By the 18th century most slave owners were beginning to realize that slavery was wrong. Many spoke out against it. (They also made excuses and tried to justify enslaving others. They knew that every ancient society had included slaves.) Many white people realized they were trapped in a bad system; they didn't know how to get out. George Washington, Thomas Jefferson, and many others wrote that slavery was evil—but they owned slaves. If you were a plantation owner and you freed your slaves, you might become poor. So

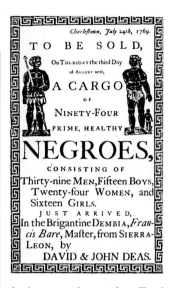

Charlestown, July 24th, 1769.

TO BE SOLD,
On Thursday the third Day of August next,
A CARGO
OF
NINETY-FOUR
PRIME, HEALTHY
NEGROES,
CONSISTING OF
Thirty-nine Men, Fifteen Boys, Twenty-four Women, and Sixteen Girls.
JUST ARRIVED,
In the Brigantine DEMBIA, Francis Bare, Master, from SIERRA-LEON, by
DAVID & JOHN DEAS.

A slave auction notice. Traders usually wanted slaves to look young and healthy—they were worth more. But they didn't like slaves who looked proud and held their heads high. Such people might be troublemakers.

Divorce, Colonial Style

Dame Alice Clawson, who lived on Virginia's eastern shore in the mid-1600s, was a woman who wouldn't take nonsense from anyone. When her husband came home from a stay with the Nanticoke Indians, he brought an Indian woman home with him. Dame Alice was outraged, and hauled her two-timing husband off to the local justices. She became the first Virginia woman to obtain a divorce.

A plantation owner *(below)*, a mansion, and rows of slave cabins—with dirt floors, no glass in the windows, no water (except a pump everyone shared), and smoky open fireplaces.

After seeing some slaves try to rebel against their owner, an observer from New Jersey wrote: "The ill Treatment which this unhappy part of mankind receives here, would almost justify them in any desperate attempt for gaining that *Civilitie*, & *Plenty* which tho' denied them, is here commonly bestowed on Horses!"

might your family. What would you do?

For a decent person, the problem was even more difficult than you can imagine. Many white Virginians had been very poor back in England or wherever they or their parents came from. Many had been let out of jail if they agreed to come to America. They knew what it was like to be oppressed, and many didn't want anything to do with slavery. But in some places it was against the law to free slaves. In some places it was against the law for black people to own land. It was against the law to teach black people to read. Many slave owners believed that if they freed their slaves, there would be no way for the slaves to survive. Most would not be able to find jobs. They might starve. They might be kidnapped and sold again into slavery.

A few whites did free their slaves. Some tried to end slavery. Most did nothing. What would you have done?

Imagine that you are a slave owner. You control other people's lives. You can order them around. You can have them whipped. You can taunt them. Do you think you might become mean and lazy? Do you think you might turn into a bad-tempered tyrant?

Some slave owners were all of those things. Some of them were among the meanest people in America's history. But there were others who felt great responsibility for their slaves.

There is a paradox connected with slavery. A *paradox* is a "puzzle." Something very puzzling happened in Colonial Virginia.

When it came time to write a constitution for our nation, it was the slave-owning Virginians who thought and wrote most about freedom. That is the paradox. Why do you think it was so?

32 The Good Life

For most of the 18th century wigs for the rich got fancier and fancier.

We haven't finished with paradoxical Virginia. We still haven't figured out why so many great leaders were growing up in that colony. Could it be that, for the very few lucky enough to be born wealthy, there was time to become well educated and time to be spent thinking?

By the 18th century, plantation owners live a privileged, lordly life. But it isn't as easy as some people think. To run a plantation well, you need to be intelligent and industrious. (In England, aristocrats often don't work—or want to work; that isn't true in America.)

Each plantation is like a small village owned by one family. That family lives in a great house with many rooms and many servants. The house is usually built of brick and has a long lawn that leads to the river. The kitchen is a separate small building. So is the laundry, the carpenter's shop, the spinning and weaving shed, the blacksmith's shed, and the plantation office.

The plantation's business is farming, which means stables and barns and a smokehouse are needed. The smokehouse is for smoking meats. (Smoking preserves meat; there are no refrigerators.) There is a dock where ships load and unload. And a shed where the cooper makes barrels. (Tobacco is packed into barrels, called

This little girl lived in Maryland. She was six years old when her picture was painted in about 1710. Her clothes might be fun to dress up in— but not for climbing trees.

121

Dancing is part of an upper-class Southern education. In the 18th century, with no TV or stereos, people have to make their own entertainment.

"hogsheads.") The plantation even has a kiln, where bricks are baked.

Slaves live in cabins built near the fields. The big plantations sometimes have 200 or more slaves. A man known as "King" Carter, the wealthiest Virginian, owns 10 plantations. Some other Virginians own two or three. All the people who live on a plantation have to eat. So they grow vegetables, corn, and wheat, and raise animals, too. Can you see why it is hard work to run a plantation well?

A plantation owner is like a business executive. He runs the plantation and sees that it makes a profit. He is responsible for the work and the workers (that means food, clothing, housing, and health care). He is probably a member of the House of Burgesses, and that means that he attends assembly sessions at the capital twice a year.

He may also be a court officer, called on to decide court cases. Besides, he and his wife give parties and entertain visitors, who sometimes stay for days and days or even weeks at a time. It is a busy life.

Plantation children don't live at all the way you do. Some of the ways they live are nice, but some you wouldn't like.

If you are a very rich planter's son you have to wear velvet pants and ruffled shirts and high-heeled shoes when company comes, just like your dad. That must be uncomfortable.

How do you like shaving your head so you can wear a powdered wig? Or wearing an embroidered cap when you play? (Only the very rich go in for head shaving.)

If you are a planter's daughter, you wear satin gowns with stiff petticoats. Now that is fun, because those are party dresses. Everyday clothing for boys and girls is more comfortable than these garments, but not

Slave or Bondman?

William Byrd was a wealthy plantation owner who compared himself to men of the Bible—the patriarchs (PAY-tree-arks). That way, he made himself believe slavery was all right. He never used the word "slave." He said "bond-man" and "bond-woman." He was using a euphemism (YOO-fuh-miz-um): a "nice" word that you use because the real word is embarrassing. (Do you know some euphemisms that we use today?) Byrd thought he lived an ideal life, and he wrote about it in his diary:

I have a large family of my own, and my Doors are open to Every Body, yet I have no Bills to pay, and half-a-Crown will rest undisturbed in my Pocket

for many Moons together. Like one of the Patriarchs, I have my Flocks and my Herds, my Bond-men and Bond-women, and every Sort of trade amongst my own Servants, so that I live in a kind of Independence from everyone but Providence.

A PLANTATION

Dock

Tobacco Barn

Wash house

Garden and Fruit Trees

Kitchen

Main House

Smokehouse

Storehouse

Office

Ice house

Slave Quarters

School house

Soap and Candle makers

Spinning & Weaving soap kettle

Shoe maker

Gardener

Black Smith

Carpenter

Carriage House

Tobacco

Stable

A plantation is self-sufficient:
it grows its own fruit and vegetables
and raises its own cows and chickens
and pigs. The money from tobacco
or cotton pays for the owners'
imported clothes and college
educations.

Bedtime Stories

Do your parents sometimes tell you to *sleep tight*? In colonial times mattresses were laid over ropes stretched between the sides of the bed frame. When the ropes sagged, they had to be tightened with a wind-up wrench. So people really meant it when they talked about sleeping tight.

How about *climbing into bed*? Do you use that expression? And do you climb into bed, or is your bed low enough so you can just fall into it? In colonial days, there was no central heating and the floor got very cold at night. So beds were tall, and most people had to actually climb a few steps to get to bed.

like the jeans and shorts that your great (lots of "greats" here!) grandchildren will wear.

One thing you do like is horseback riding. Everyone rides horses, and everyone learns to dance, too.

If you are the child of plantation owners, you have your own schoolteacher who lives with you. Life is good to you. You study and play and go to parties. You eat big meals of meats and pies and vegetables, all home cooked. Slaves pick up after you. How do you treat them? Some boys and girls are considerate; some are not.

If you are smart and study hard, you will be taught to read the Bible in the languages in which it was written. You will learn about ancient Rome and its gladiators, poets, and politicians. You will

Rigorous means "tough" or "demanding."

A *patrician* is an aristocrat, someone of high social rank. "Patrician" can be a noun or an adjective

play a musical instrument. Many Americans born after you will not have as rigorous an education.

It is a patrician life, full of special privileges. If you are a boy you may finish your schooling at Virginia's College of William and Mary or perhaps at college in England. Someday you will be expected to serve as a representative of your neighbors in the House of Burgesses. Your parents and teachers are training you to be a leader.

The College of William and Mary in Williamsburg was named for England's king and queen and was the second college in the colonies.

Even if she hates it, every little girl has to learn to sew and embroider. Girls practice on samplers like this one—it includes 12 different kinds of stitches.

33 Virginia's Capital

Virginia's enterprising Governor Alexander Spotswood started an iron industry and explored the Shenandoah Valley.

Do you remember the mosquitoes, deerflies, and snakes at Jamestown, back in John Smith's time? Well, things got better on that swampy peninsula—but not a lot better. In 1676 some frontiersmen, led by Nathaniel Bacon, marched to Jamestown. They had asked for help fighting Indians and didn't get it. They hated the governor, Sir William Berkeley (BARK-lee), who was a tyrant. Even the king called him "an old fool." The rebels burned the State House.

Almost as soon as the State House was rebuilt, it burned down again. This time it may have been an accident. Still, in 1699, when someone suggested moving the Virginia capital to Middle Plantation—eight miles away but on higher ground—most people thought it a fine idea.

Actually there were at least two "someones" who did the suggesting. One was James Blair, a Scotsman who was minister of Bruton Parish Church, the Anglican church at Middle Plantation. Reverend Blair was also the founder and first president of the College of William and Mary, which was at Middle Plantation. The other someone was Francis Nicholson, the new royal governor. Nicholson agreed that with a church and college in place, Middle Plantation would be a capital spot for the capital. But Middle Plantation wasn't much of a name for a town. A new name was needed. The king of England's name was a natural choice, and the town became Williamsburg.

That little town, born at the beginning of the 18th century, danced across the stage of history for about 80 years. Then it left the spotlight and was forgotten (until the 20th century, when it was restored and rebuilt as if it were still in the 1700s).

Governor Berkeley was a rich, selfish old man who taxed the small planters heavily. Some planters needed help. The Indians, fighting for their land, were attacking frontier farms.

Nathaniel Bacon had two plantations. One of them, near where Richmond is today, was on the edge of Indian territory. Indians attacked, killed an overseer, stole cattle, and burned tobacco. When the governor wouldn't help, Bacon led a small army against the Indians. Berkeley was furious. He gathered soldiers and planned to fight Bacon and his rebels. Bacon's army marched on Jamestown. The governor and his men ran to a warship and sailed off. Bacon burned the town and started his own government. Then he got sick and died. Berkeley came back and hanged all of Bacon's followers. This is called Bacon's Rebellion.

JOSEPH KIDD,

Upholsterer, in Williamsburg.

HANGS rooms with paper or damask, stuffs sophas, couches, and chairs, in the neatest manner, makes all forts of bed furniture, window curtains, and matrasses, and fits carpets to any room with the greatest exactness. — N. B. He will go to Gentlemens houses in the country to perform any of the above articles.

At his LEAD MANUFACTORY, behind the church, may be had all forts of sheet lead, pipes for conveying water from the tops of houses, cisterns, milk pans (which will keep milk sweet and cool in the height of summer) still worms made and mended, every other article in the plumbing business.

He also undertakes all forts of HOUSE PAINTING, GILD... and GLAZING and paints floor cloths, chimney boards, ...t, according ... rections.

Lord Botetourt, a popular English governor, was the first to fully occupy the Williamsburg governor's palace *(above)*. His groom of the chambers, Joseph Kidd, started his own decorating business.

The word **crown**, as it is used here, means the British government.

Jamestown's landowners didn't think moving the capital was a good idea, but most of the other plantation owners did.

Francis Nicholson arrived in Williamsburg fresh from Maryland, where he had been governor and had designed Maryland's capital, the bustling port of Annapolis. He was eager to plan Williamsburg, and he did it with care, using new ideas from France.

Williamsburg was "laid out regularly in lots…sufficient each for a house and garden and…free passage for the air which is grateful in violent hot weather." Wide, tree-lined Duke of Gloucester Street ran down the middle of the town, with the Capitol at one end and the college's Wren Building at the other end. Bruton Parish Church, with its white spire, stood proudly on the same street, along with neat houses, shops, and a grassy mall. Overlooking the mall was the finest building in the colony: the handsome, stately governor's palace. Now picture people, horses, cows, sheep, and gardens, and you have an idea of Williamsburg.

If you stand outside the governor's palace and look at the brick fence—with its stone British unicorn on top and fancy iron gates—you will be impressed. If you are lucky you may get invited inside for a musical evening. You'll sit in the candlelit ballroom, where men in starched linen blouses and women in silk brocade gowns smile and nod at each other. A display of muskets and swords in the entry is intended to leave you awed with the Crown's military might.

But, best of all, most young people agree, is a chance to lose yourself in the boxwood maze garden growing behind the palace. Almost everyone knows the ancient myth of the maze and the monstrous Minotaur on the island of Crete. The maze behind the governor's palace doesn't have any monsters—there are some peacocks strutting around—but people like to go in it and pretend they are lost, especially if there are two of them and they are in love.

Most of the year, Williamsburg is a sleepy village of 2,000 souls. Half of them are African-Americans. But in April and October, when the House of Burgesses and the courts are in session, the population doubles. Men sleep three to a bed at Christiana Campbell's tavern, where the good Mrs. Campbell, "a little old Woman, about four feet high & equally thick," keeps a popular dining room.

These are Public Times, and people come to take care of colonial business, make laws, consider court cases, see friends, and shop. You can buy a wig at the wig makers, a violin at the music shop, or a gingerbread cookie at the bakery. If you want "to put on the dog," you can have dog-hide shoes made for you at the boot makers. You

might go to an auction, a horse race, or a fair. You can see a play. (The first theater in the English colonies opens in 1717.)

One traveler writes of Williamsburg, "At the time of the assemblies and general courts, it is crowded with the gentry of the country. On those occasions there are balls and other amusements; but as soon as business is finished, they return to their plantations

The Reverend Blair didn't like fun and games, but he took charge of William and Mary and made it a good place to go to college.

Cooks at work in a big 18th-century kitchen like that of the governor's mansion. Dinners were huge and often consisted of a dozen courses or more—with fish, beef, and turkey all in the same meal.

and the town is in a manner deserted."

For most people a trip to Williamsburg means having a good time—unless the Reverend Mr. Blair happens to come by. Blair doesn't have a sense of humor. For 50 long years, he is a powerful force in the community. It is said that three governors have been recalled to London because of his complaints. A fourth governor remembered him as "a very vile old fellow." Blair usually gets his way.

And his way is not one of tolerance. A landowning aristocracy rules Virginia and outsiders remain outside. Only Anglicans can be elected burgesses. A plan for religious liberty is hatched in Williamsburg in the second half of the 18th century, but it might not have happened if Reverend Blair had been alive.

But Blair is mortal and not typical of most Virginians. The Virginia way is gracious and courtly and easygoing. William and Mary's wise law professor, George Wythe (say *with*), will soon come to prominence in Williamsburg. He is kind

School's Out

Virginia's governor Alexander Spotswood wanted to be friends with the Indians. He sponsored the Indian Act of 1714. It created an outpost where the colonists could meet and trade with Indians. An English school was founded to teach Indian children about Christianity and English ways.

Many colonists were angry about Spotswood's ideas. Some didn't want anything to do with Native Americans. Others were afraid the Indians would sell their furs to Virginia's governor and not to them. In 1717, at the colonists' urging, the king repealed the Indian Act. The outpost and Indian school were closed.

and considerate and learned; some people call him "a walking library." George Wythe becomes mayor of Williamsburg. He frees his slaves long before he dies. He hates slavery. One of his favorite students is a young man named Thomas Jefferson.

If you had a magic wand that could waft you anywhere, you might consider landing at the Raleigh Tavern in Williamsburg on a day when George Washington, Thomas Jefferson, Patrick Henry, and Peyton Randolph are having a conversation. Just sit back and listen. Those Virginians and their friends have a rare talent for good times and serious thought. They are as splendid and energetic a group of leaders as any nation has ever produced.

They are struggling with a weighty problem: how to create a new and fair government on this gorgeous continent. And they are being pulled in two directions. There are many who think as James Blair does and want to reproduce Old England in America. One professor at the College of William and Mary writes approvingly that people in Williamsburg "behave themselves exactly like the gentry in London."

But there are others who don't behave like English gentry. They have come to America because they are unhappy with the Old World and its society of rigid classes. They want to try something new, in what they call the New World. This little village of Williamsburg will ring with debates on the purposes of government. Should individual liberty be the goal? Or is it better to preserve an orderly community where everyone has a sure place? What does "the consent of the governed" really mean? Wouldn't you like to hear what Thomas Jefferson and George Washington have to say about those questions?

George Wythe, who became one of the original signers of the Declaration of Independence, had very little proper education when he was growing up. But, with only the help of his mother, he taught himself Greek, Latin, philosophy, mathematics, and science. He even got a rabbi to teach him Hebrew.

The colonists who wanted to teach Indians didn't give up. This Indian school opened at the College of William and Mary in 1723. About a dozen Indians at a time lived and studied there. Today, the building is still in use as part of the college.

34 Pretend Some More

Silversmiths also made pewter items, like this tankard with its flip-up lid.

Venerate means "respect." A farmer's plow was the most important machine he owned.

You are 10 years old and indentured to Patrick Beech, a silversmith in Williamsburg. Beech was a real silversmith, we know that, but we don't know much about his servants and apprentices. We do know about the jobs they would have done and the way they might have lived. So you can pretend to be one of them. If you do, you will get an idea of what life was like for some children in the 18th century.

You have been in Virginia just a year. Your parents died of influenza in London. Since you had nowhere to go and no money, the Lord Mayor sent you and some other orphans to Virginia. Sometimes you are homesick for your friends in London, but you are beginning to like it in America. Life isn't easy, but it is better than it was in London.

Beech keeps you working from before the sun comes up until dark. Your first job in the morning is to light a fire to warm the house and another to heat the forge where silver is melted and formed. Then you clean the kitchen, run errands, and sometimes do odd jobs in the silver shop. You don't get time to play, and lately you have begun to hate Mr. Beech. He never seems to smile.

Mrs. Beech has taught you to read. She takes you to church and whips you when you are bad. She does the same with her children. She is fair but very busy. You miss your own mother.

But you do have a friend in the silver shop. His name is Tom, and he was apprenticed to a watchmaker in London before he came to the colonies. Tom says Beech is not a bad man, just worried. There isn't enough work in Williamsburg. There are too many silversmiths, and the rich planters buy their good silver in England. So Beech must make silver teeth and set them in people's mouths. He repairs watches and makes clocks, and sometimes silver cups and trays and jewelry. He has a big family to feed, along with his servants. There is enough food, but nothing extra.

Neither you nor Tom is free. The law says you must stay with Patrick Beech until you are 21. Tom is also an indentured servant. Beech paid for his passage from London: he must work for him for five years. Then, Tom tells you, he will go to Charles Town and open his own shop. He has heard the planters in South Carolina are very rich.

More than anything, you want to hunt and fish and learn to use a rifle. You have seen enough of the silversmith's work—fires and forges, pouring liquid metal, hammering silver into shape, putting teeth into the jaws of people who scream in pain. You need to be patient. Someday you will have everything you wish for—and more.

Now, pretend again. This time you are the child of a Virginia farmer. You live in a small wooden house with a big fireplace at one end. The house has only one big room with a sleeping loft. At night your parents sleep in front of the fire with the baby, and you and your brothers climb a ladder to the loft. You all sleep on straw mattresses.

The only clothes you have are those you wear, and a Sunday shirt. Tobacco and corn grow poorly on your land, because it is worn out. You have enough food, but you don't eat a balanced diet. You are sometimes sick, and you will die when you are 40.

Still, you are luckier than many children. You have had a year of schooling, and you know how to read. Your parents hope your life will be better than theirs. And it will be. At 15 you will head out to the western frontier, where you will find land and opportunity. Your schooling will help you succeed. You will marry, have 10 children, and own land enough for all of them to farm.

Most poor white boys and girls don't get to school. And there are no schools for black children. Many 18th-century Southern children never learn to read or write. It is difficult to have schools when people live so far apart on farms. It is difficult to have churches, too. Some ministers ride horseback from one church to another. The law

Forty Shillings Reward.

RAN away this morning from the fubfcriber, an Apprentice BOY named James Hoy, near 18 years old. about 5 feet 8 inches high, fair complexion, and hair tied behind. He took with him a brown jean coat, grey furtout, new fhoes, round felt hat, and many other articles of cloathing.——Whoever brings him back or confines him in gaol, fo that he be had again, fhall receive the above reward.

JOHN FARRAN.

Philadelphia, June 26.   3fp

This is a pewter works. Pewter, which is a mixture of tin, lead, and copper or bismuth, was for people who couldn't afford silver. The apprentice is turning the wheel that drives the bellows to keep the furnace hot. If the 'prentice got fed up and ran away, his master would offer a reward for bringing him back. In the colonies, even unskilled laborers were hard to find.

No one knows who painted this picture, but it may have been done in South Carolina. The slaves may be celebrating a wedding by "jumping the broomstick." Some of their clothes look like those worn in Yoruba, which is in Nigeria in Africa. The banjo-like instrument *(above)* resembles a Yoruban *molo*; the other instrument looks like an African *gudu-gudu*.

Hoeing Cotton

From the story of a former slave, Solomon Northup:

About the first of July, when [the cotton] is a foot high or thereabouts, it is hoed the fourth and last time....During all these hoeings the overseer or driver follows the slaves on horseback with a whip.... The fastest hoer takes the lead row. He is usually about a rod in front of his companions. If one of them passes him, he is whipped. If one falls behind or is a moment idle, he is whipped. In fact, the lash is flying from morning until night.

says you must go to the Anglican church every Sunday.

Your parents hate that law, and another law that makes them pay taxes to help support the Anglican Church. They say the Anglican Church is for rich folks. They would like to join the Baptist church, but they can get in trouble if they do that. A law says their children could be taken from them if they join a free-thinking church. Since you are one of their children you agree that is a terrible law. Actually, it isn't enforced very often. Perhaps the law is meant to scare people away from new churches: like those of the Baptists and Methodists and New Light Presbyterians.

Belonging to that Anglican Church of England, as most Virginians do, makes you different from people in Massachusetts. Virginians love England and English clothing, paintings, furnishings, and ideas. They feel closer to people in England than they do to those in New England.

Now pretend that you are a slave. You don't want to? You are right. No one wants to be a slave. Some slaves, especially those who work in the fields on some big plantations, live in small huts and sleep on old blankets piled on the dirt floor. They don't eat well and they work almost all the time. Other slaves, especially those who are house servants, live in small wooden houses with beds and tables and furnishings that come from the plantation workshop or, sometimes, from the big house. Visitors from Europe will say they live better than most peasants in the Old World. (Which is probably why so many European peasants want to come to America.)

Your name is Sarah, and you live on a farm in North Carolina. There are 18 of you slaves (including children) in four families and you share two houses near the tobacco fields. A fireplace divides each house in half. Your house has a front porch, as many houses do in Africa. The porch is a nice place to rest on a hot evening. You have your own garden, which provides corn and greens and potatoes. They have made you strong and healthy. You are 11, and you can't read and never will be taught how. But you can sing and play the banjo, and that makes you popular in church. Your faith is important to you and your family. You are Christians, and you have brought your African spirituality to that religion.

35 South Carolina: Riches, Rice, Slaves

The seal of the Carolinas viewed Indians more kindly than most colonists did.

The Carolinas, North and South, were granted to eight lords proprietors by King Charles II. The lords never meant to live in America, and they didn't. They just planned to get rich by using the Carolinas to produce three products that were expensive in England: wine, silk, and olive oil.

The Carolinas worked out, but not as the lords had expected. Indigo, a plant grown for its blue dye, and rice became principal crops—not wine, silk, or olive oil. Eventually the colonies were bought back by the king. The lords lost out, and the Carolinas became royal colonies.

In South Carolina, Charles Town, named for Charles II, prospered from its beginning. No longer were there terrible starving and dying times when a colony was founded. Jamestown and Plymouth had taught the colonists what not to do.

Charleston (which was the name Charles Town turned into) soon became the busiest port in the South. It attracted younger sons of the English nobility, who gave it an aristocratic flavor.

Many of Charleston's leaders came from the tiny island of Barbados in the Caribbean Sea. In the 17th century Barbados was the wealthiest and most crowded of all English American colonies. (In 1680 Barbados's exports were more valuable

Unlike Boston or New Amsterdam, Charleston's and Philadelphia's streets were planned before any houses were built.

133

Here Peter Manigault, a well-known Charleston Huguenot, seems to be drinking too much. (He's the one holding a bottle on the left.) Drinking was sometimes a problem in early America. (Is it today?)

One Man's View

In 1769 "Capt. Martin a Man of War" wrote this poem about Charleston:

Black and white all mix'd together,
Inconstant, strange, unhealthful weather,
Burning heat and chilling cold
Dangerous both to young and old
Boisterous winds and heavy rains
Fevers and rheumatic pains
Agues plenty without doubt
Sores, boils, the prickling heat and gout
Musquitos on the skin make blotches
Centipedes and large cockroaches
Frightful creatures in the waters
Porpoises, sharks and alligators
Houses built on barren land
No lamps or lights, but streets of sand
Pleasant walks, if you can find 'em
Scandalous tongues, if any mind 'em
The markets dear and little money
Large potatoes, sweet as honey
Water bad, past all drinking
Men and women without thinking
Every thing at a high price
But rum, hominy and rice
Many a widow not unwilling
Many a beau not worth a shilling
Many a bargain, if you strike it
This is Charles-town, how do you like it.

than the exports of all of the North American mainland.)

South Carolina had to find ways to attract settlers. One way was to practice religious tolerance. Religious wars were making people flee from Europe. The Carolinas welcomed them, and that led to an interesting mix of peoples. Scots settled on the coast and helped fight off Spanish attacks. French Protestants, called Huguenots (HUE-guh-nots), came and proved to be just the kind of colonists the new land needed. In France they were persecuted, but France's shortsightedness was America's good fortune. The Huguenots were carpenters and blacksmiths and masons, and they believed in hard work. What John Smith would have given to have had them in Jamestown!

Field-workers were needed to plant and harvest the rice that was making the colony rich. The settlers from Barbados were used to owning slaves; they wanted slaves in America, and they encouraged it. It is an irony that Africans probably taught the white settlers how to cultivate rice, because it was rice that made slavery profitable in South Carolina. Soon there were more black people in South Carolina than whites.

South Carolina became an aristocratic colony with a few very wealthy people holding almost all the economic and political power. It was different from the other

Southern colonies in many ways, but especially because it had that important city: Charleston. In Virginia and North Carolina there was no great city. For most of the year, plantation folk in those colonies lived isolated lives. That was not the case in South Carolina. Some plantation owners in South Carolina visited their plantations only occasionally. They spent their time in Charleston, where they lived in big houses and went to fancy parties.

The Huguenots mixed and married with the English; their tastes and ideas helped create the most elegant society in the colonies.

Those who were wealthy thought life in Charleston finer than in any place on earth. But the majority of Charlestonians were not wealthy. The majority of South Carolinians were not free. They were Africans, and they worked as field hands, craftspeople, and servants. But they had their own ideas and traditions, and they brought those African ideas, songs, stories, and habits to their new home. After a while, some of those African ideas became mixed with ideas they found in America. Brer Rabbit, who started as an African, became American. In South Carolina African-Americans developed their own language, Gullah.

Some people in South Carolina speak Gullah today. They talk quickly, without a Southern accent. Gullah combines words from English, French, and a number of African languages. You may have heard some Gullah words, such as *goober* (peanut), *gumbo* (soup with okra), *juke* (as in jukebox), and *voodoo* (witchcraft). Here is a sentence in Gullah: *Shishuh tall pass una*. It means "Sister is taller than you."

"Whether the province may have acquired it [rice] by shipwreck, or whether it may have been carried there with slaves, or whether it be sent from England, it is certain that the soil is favorable to it," said a visitor.

In 1775, Charleston was the fourth-biggest city in the colonies, with a population of 12,000. The biggest of all was Philadelphia, with 40,000 people. It was bigger than any English city except London.

These are indigo farmworkers. Indigo was an ideal second crop because it needs no work in winter, when all the hard labor of rice planting must be done. The blue dye made from the indigo plant was much prized.

36 North Carolina: Dissenters and Pirates

William Byrd *didn't think much of his neighbors in North Carolina. This is what he wrote about them:* "Both Cattle and Hogs ramble in the Neighbouring Marshes and Swamps, where they maintain themselves the whole winter long, and are not fetch'd home till the spring…and many of the poor Creatures perish in the Mire….These people live so much upon Swine's flesh, that it…makes them extremely hoggish in their Temper, & many…seem to Grunt rather than to speak."

Many Southerners didn't want to be Anglicans. This is a Lutheran church.

North Carolina was different. It had tough land to tame, so its settlers were apt to be free-spirited small farmers. Many were outcasts and religious dissenters from aristocratic Virginia. In Virginia the rich landholders were in control, and they were Anglicans. People who wanted to join the new religious sects—the Baptists and the Methodists—were persecuted in Virginia. Some moved south to North Carolina.

North Carolina may have been the most democratic of all the colonies. Generally, North Carolinians minded their own business and left their neighbors alone, which may be why pirates made the North Carolina coast a base for their adventuring. Although some said it was because the pirates paid the North Carolina governor to leave them alone. That could be true, because it was finally a force from Virginia that got Blackbeard—the most famous and ferocious of the pirates. His real name was Edward Teach. He braided his great black beard into pigtails, wove ribbons into them,

Right: How an artist imagined Blackbeard and his ruffians enjoying themselves at their Carolina hideout. There were women who liked the pirate life, too.

and then hung smoking pieces of rope from his hat. At night the pigtails looked like coiling snakes, and the burning rope gave his face a glowing, eerie look. It was enough to scare anyone, and it did scare a lot of sailors.

Anne Bonney scared them, too. She was a tough pirate who sailed the Caribbean and Carolina coast, and had no trouble terrorizing seamen.

In 1677 some North Carolinians rebelled against England. They didn't like England's Navigation Acts, which forced them to pay

Genuine women pirates: Mary Read *(left)* and Anne Bonney. They were friends who survived a death sentence.

The Death of Blackbeard

In 1718 Blackbeard stationed his ship in Pamlico Sound off the North Carolina coast. No ship was permitted to pass through without paying the pirate a bribe. Governor Spotswood of Virginia decided to do something about that. He offered £100 reward for the pirate. Lieutenant Robert Maynard sailed south. In a ferocious battle, "Blackbeard received a shot in his body...yet he stood his ground and fought with great fury till he received five and twenty wounds. ...At length, as he was cocking another pistol...he fell down dead." Maynard, to prove he had killed Blackbeard, cut off the pirate's head, stuck it on his bowsprit, and sailed home.

An enterprising 12-year-old boy read about Blackbeard's death and Maynard's heroism. He was so captivated by the story that he wrote a long poem about it, set it in type, printed it on sheets of paper, and sold it in the streets of Boston. Here are the last lines:

*When the bloody fight
    was over,
we're informed by
    a Letter writ,
Teach's head was
    made a Cover
to the Jack Staff
    of the Ship:
Thus they sailed
    to Virginia,
and when the Story told,
How they killed the
    Pirates many,
they'd Applause from
    young and old.*

Can you guess the name of that boy who wrote the poem about Blackbeard on the previous page? He was a printer who became a scientist and a statesman.

A: Benjamin Franklin!

Pirate fun could be nasty. Here, pirates make captured friars give them piggyback rides, a shipboard sport called "monk-riding." One pirate wields a cat-o'-nine-tails, a cruel whip common on ships.

In 1997, some divers found a wreck off the coast of North Carolina. There were nine cannons on board, and others scattered on the ocean floor. Archaeologists believe it is Blackbeard's ship, *Queen Anne's Revenge.*

taxes to England on goods sold to other colonies. If a North Carolina tobacco grower sold some of his tobacco to a merchant in Boston, he was supposed to pay a tax to England. Did that make any sense? The colonists didn't think so.

Some North Carolinians refused to pay. They even set up their own government and tried to get free of England. They almost got away with it. They put British officials in jail, elected a legislature, and chose their leader, John Culpeper, as governor. For two years they exercised all the powers and duties of government. But the British finally got angry. They tried Culpeper for treason. He was convicted but not punished—maybe because he was so popular.

One hundred years later, in 1776, people in all the colonies were angry about English taxes. The colonists would unite, as Popé had united the Pueblo Indians—and…well, you'll see what happened.

Pieces of Eight

Money wasn't simple in colonial times. Every country had its own kind of *currency*—coins and paper money—just as they do today. So English coins, Dutch coins, French coins, Spanish coins, and Portuguese coins were all *circulating*—being used for buying and selling. That wasn't all. Colonial governments were minting coins, and private banks were, too. And even with all these different bodies making coins, there still weren't enough—so people sometimes cut them up into bits and pieces if they needed change. Paper bills weren't much used—most people preferred money made of a metal that had value, like silver or copper. (The coins we have today that we call silver and copper don't contain much of those metals. But in the 17th century they did.)

The Spanish *real* (it means "royal" in Spanish) was widely used; it became the basis for the dollar in America. Those *reales* were often cut into eight pieces. Have you read the book *Treasure Island* by Robert Louis Stevenson? The parrot that belongs to the villain of that adventure story is named Captain Flint, and he is always squawking the phrase "Pieces of eight!" Pieces of eight were eventually coins in their own right, but they began as cut-up pieces of a *real*.

That is also the reason a quarter is sometimes called *two bits*. And that Spanish heritage explains why the New York Stock Exchange quoted fractional stock prices in eighths of a dollar until January 2001 when, finally, they changed to decimals with the penny as a base.

Top: Blackbeard's head swings from the bowsprit of Lieutenant Maynard's ship. The cast bronze bell *(above)* is part of Blackbeard's treasure recovered in 1997 from his ship, *Queen Anne's Revenge.* *Left:* an archaeologist raises one of Blackbeard's cannons from the sea floor. His ship had more than 40 cannons; divers have found 13 of them.

37 Royal Colonies and a No-Blood Revolution

Sir Edmund Andros wouldn't even let the people of Cape Cod keep the oil they got from stranded whales. Whales were "royal fish."

I hope you don't mind, but here is some more English history. It is the year 1686 (what century is that?), and James II is king of England. You met him before, when he was the Duke of York and his brother, King Charles II, gave him New York and New Jersey.

Now Charles is dead and James wears the crown. Unfortunately, James is not the nicest of kings. And it doesn't help that he is a Catholic, because most people in England belong to the Church of England.

King James II would like to rule without Parliament. He wants to be an "absolute monarch." He believes, as did his father, Charles I, that kings have a "divine right" to rule. That means he thinks God wants him to be king. He would like to make England Roman Catholic again. He will learn that you can't force religion on people.

James tries to take charge in America, too. Before his time, the English kings hadn't bothered much with America. The colonists were mostly left alone. Now, King James wants to change that, so he sends Sir Edmund Andros to New England. Andros is a tough, take-control person who tries to tell the Puritans how to run their colony.

It is hard to tell a Puritan anything. The New England Puritans came to America to run their own affairs, and they don't want an outsider making rules for them—especially Andros. They think he is a bully.

Finally, a mob goes after Andros. He is scared. You would be, too—mobs are dangerous. Andros puts on a woman's dress and tries to escape—oops!—he forgot to change his boots. Women don't wear heavy boots. Andros is spotted and captured. The Bostonians cool down and ship him back to England.

The king is annoyed with the troublesome colonists in America.

They won't behave as they are told. But now King James has too many problems to worry much about the colonies. In England things are heating up. The English people have had enough of James II. They have another revolution—a civilized revolution. "You're not king anymore, James," is what they say. Since James isn't killed—as his father was in the English Civil War of 1649—this revolution, in 1688, is called the "Bloodless" or "Glorious Revolution." It proves that revolutions don't have to be violent.

James's Protestant daughter, Mary, and her Dutch husband, William of Orange, are asked to be rulers. They are the couple the Virginians honored when they named the College of William and Mary.

The revolution is glorious because the English people make a deal with the new king and queen. They insist that Parliament have more power than the monarchs. They also demand a Bill of Rights for the people. It is a terrible time for absolute monarchs, but a great moment for freedom. In America, the colonists find it inspiring.

Read that last paragraph again. It's important to remember that *the Glorious Revolution gave Parliament more power than the king. HOORAY!*

Do you think that makes things better for the colonies? Well, sometimes parliaments can be as pesky as kings.

When the English parliament begins to make rules for the American colonies, the colonists will get annoyed. The Americans will complain that Parliament is too powerful, especially when Parliament ignores Massachusetts's beloved charter and makes the state a royal colony with a royal governor.

The grumbling that begins in New England in 1691 will start the colonists thinking about having their own glorious revolution. They will have one—but it will not be bloodless.

Do you think that the English Bill of Rights served as an inspiration for what was to come in America?

A king and queen who helped make a peaceful revolution.

In 1687 Connecticut's charter was hidden in this Hartford oak tree to keep it out of Andros's hands. The tree blew down in 1856 and everyone who could cut a piece for a souvenir.

38 A Nasty Triangle

Men are loaded onto a slaver (slave ship) and chained together at the ankles.

You may be getting the idea that the United States began as a collection of settlements that were not much alike. And you are right.

South Carolina wasn't like Pennsylvania, and Maryland wasn't like Connecticut. The people who founded the colonies had a lot to do with those differences, and so did the conditions of the land.

Massachusetts had a special problem because of its rocky soil and cold climate. It was tough being a farmer in New England, but New Englanders were tough people who liked challenges. So they did farm, although for many it was "subsistence farming." That means they grew enough for themselves; they didn't usually have extra crops to sell. A few New England farmers were able to sell their farm products abroad but, mostly, New England's land just wasn't right for large farms—or plantations—like those in the South.

And when it came to industry, the British made things difficult. They wouldn't let the colonists manufacture goods that competed with English goods. You can understand why that caused some grumbling.

New Englanders had to find ways to earn a living. Fishing was one way. Cod became New England's gold, just as tobacco was

The people in this shed are cleaning and drying codfish, which was (and still is) an important trading commodity for New England.

The New England lumber mill cuts and splits the logs and spits them straight into the river so they can float down to the towns and ship-yards that need them for building houses and boats.

Virginia's. The Puritan settlers caught codfish and then salted and shipped and sold the fish in Europe or the Caribbean Islands. In order to do that, they needed ships. So they became shipbuilders. To make ships they needed lumber. So they harvested timber and began selling wood and wood products. They became merchants carrying goods around the world. Yankee ships were familiar sights in Singapore and Rangoon and Bristol. And New England boys, who hung around the wharfs, got a chance to touch Dutch coins, Chinese silks, or fruit from Spain. They heard tales of adventures in Tripoli and Jamaica and dreamed of becoming skippers and going to faraway places themselves.

Soon Yankees were trading all kinds of things. They might take their salted cod to Barbados and trade it for cane sugar. Then they'd go to Virginia to pick up tobacco. They'd take the tobacco and sugar to England and trade them for cash, guns, and English cloth. Then on to Africa, where they exchanged the guns and cloth for men, women, and children. From there it was back across the Atlantic Ocean to the West Indies, where the people were sold into slavery. Finally they sailed home to New England (or, sometimes, New York or Annapolis). All that was called the "triangular trade." It made some people very rich.

Between 1526 and 1870, nearly 10 million slaves were shipped from Africa to:

Europe
175,000

Spanish America
1,552,000

Brazil
3,647,000

British Caribbean
1,665,000

British North America and the United States
399,000

French America
1,600,000

Dutch America
500,000

Danish West Indies
28,000

MEN'S ROOM.   BOYS' ROOM.   WOMEN'S ROOM.

This drawing of the slave ship *Brookes* caused an uproar. It led, in 1788, to a British law limiting the number of slaves per ship's ton. The drawing was not quite accurate, but close enough: conditions were horrendous. Death rates varied, but perhaps 20% of the captured people died on shipboard in the early 17th century. The death rate for crew members—from beatings and disease—was often higher. Those who owned the slave ships sat home in comfort and profited.

Picture a triangle—a long one. Do you have three points in your mind? Now stretch the triangle across the Atlantic Ocean. Put one point on the New England coast, another in Africa, and the third in South Carolina. Are you sure you have that clearly in your mind? Now imagine a boat sailing along that triangle, from New England to Africa to South Carolina, and back to New England.

Stretch another triangle across the Atlantic. This one can start in England, go to Africa, and have a third point in Virginia. The Atlantic Ocean was once filled with ships sailing triangular routes. Most of them included a stop in the West Indies. (They were very jagged triangles; a few were rectangles.)

Let's pretend a triangle is starting at Newport, Rhode Island (near Boston). You can watch as a ship is loaded with rum and guns. (Rum is an alcoholic drink made from sugarcane.) The ship heads for Africa, where the rum and guns will be traded for African people.

The Africans have been captured by enemy tribesmen and sold to African slave traders. The slave traders bargain with the New England boat captain, who buys as many people as he can squeeze on his ship. Some of the captives are children, kidnapped from their parents.

Olaudah Equiano was one of those children. He was 11 in 1756, when he was captured in Benin. He was the youngest of seven children, a happy boy in a loving home. Like many other prosperous African families, his family had slaves. Imagine that you are Olaudah as you read his words:

One day, when all our people were gone out to their works as usual, and only I and my sister were left to mind the house, two men and a woman got over our walls, and in a moment seized us both; and without giving us time to cry out or to make any resistance, they stopped our mouths and ran off with us into the nearest wood. Here they tied our hands, and continued to carry us as far as they could, till night came

Born Free

In a graveyard at Concord, Massachusetts, stands a stone carved thus:

God wills us free—
  man wills us slaves
I will as God wills:
  Gods will be done.
Here lies the body of
  John Jack
A native of Africa
  who died March 1773,
  aged about sixty years.
Tho born in the land
  of slavery
He was born free:
Tho he lived in a land
  of liberty
He lived a slave

Till by his honest
  tho stolen labours
He acquired
  the source of slavery
Which gave him his freedom:
Tho not long before
  Death the great Tyrant
Gave him his final
  emancipation
And put him on a footing
  with kings.
Tho a slave to vice
He practised those virtues
Without which kings are
  but slaves.

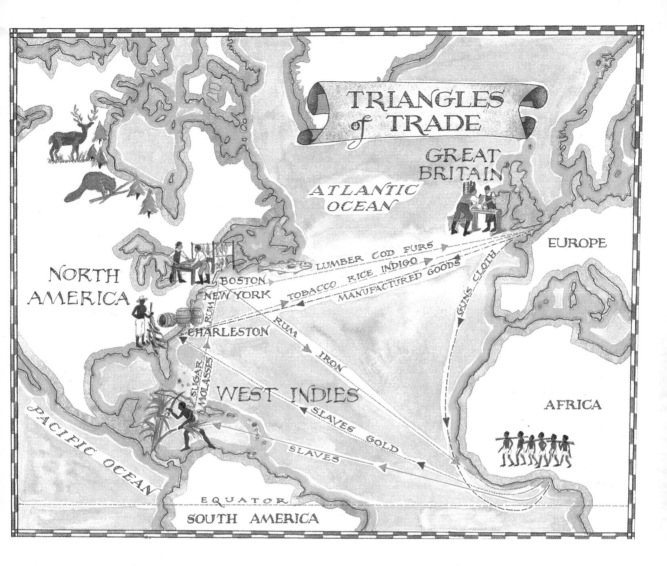

TRIANGLES of TRADE

GREAT BRITAIN

ATLANTIC OCEAN

EUROPE

NORTH AMERICA

LUMBER COD FURS

TOBACCO RICE INDIGO

MANUFACTURED GOODS

GUNS CLOTH

BOSTON

NEW YORK

RUM

CHARLESTON

RUM

IRON

SUGAR MOLASSES

WEST INDIES

SLAVES GOLD

AFRICA

SLAVES

PACIFIC OCEAN

EQUATOR

SOUTH AMERICA

on, when we reached a small house, where the robbers halted for re-freshment and spent the night.

Olaudah and his sister are taken on a long journey, separated, and sold. He is passed from person to person, staying a month here, a few weeks there. Olaudah sees many parts of Africa and has many adventures. He tries to run away but is unsuccessful. Then, for the first time in his life, he sees the ocean.

The first object which saluted my eyes when I arrived on the coast was the sea, and a slaveship, which was then riding at anchor and waiting for its cargo. These filled me with astonishment, which was soon converted into terror....When I was carried on board I was immediately handled, and tossed up to see if I was sound, by some of the crew; and I was now persuaded that I had got into a world of bad spirits, and that they were going to kill me.

There was more than one trade triangle. But all of them were tied up with slavery, and slavery was tied up with them. Most of the people who made money out of slavery didn't want to see it come to an end.

Olaudah is tossed below deck, where the smell is so bad he becomes sick and cannot eat. When he refuses food he is tied down and beaten. Frightened, he is at first unable to talk to anyone because the other Africans do not speak his language. Finally he meets some men who speak the language of Benin.

> I asked them if these people had no country, but lived in this hollow place [the ship]. They told me they did not, but came from a distant one....I then asked where were their women? Had they any like themselves? I was told they had. "And why," said I, "do we not see them?" They answered because they were left behind. I asked how the vessel could go? They told me they could not tell; but that there was cloth put upon the masts by the help of ropes I saw, and then the vessel went on; and the white men had some spell or magic they put in the water, when they liked, in order to stop the vessel. I was exceedingly amazed at this account, and really thought they were spirits.

Olaudah learns that he is being taken to the white men's country to work.

> I then was a little revived, and thought, if it were no worse than working, my situation was not so desperate: but still I feared I should be put to death, the white people looked and acted, as I thought, in so savage a manner; for I had never seen among any people such instances of brutal cruelty; and this is not only shown towards us blacks, but also to some of the whites themselves. One white man in particular I saw, when we were permitted to be on deck, flogged so unmercifully with a large rope near the foremast, that he died in consequence of it; and they tossed him over the side as they would have done a brute. This made me fear these people the more; and I expected nothing less than to be treated in the same manner.

Olaudah describes the scene belowdecks, where people are packed so closely they can hardly turn over. The smells, he says, are "loathsome." Women shriek, the dying groan, all is "a scene of horror."

> One day, when we had a smooth sea and moderate wind, two of my wearied countrymen, who were chained together (I was near them at the time), preferring death to such a life of misery, somehow made through the nettings, and jumped into the sea.

Olaudah is taken to Barbados in the West Indies, where he is sold. His story is different from most. He will go to sea as a slave, have many adventures, learn to read, and write his autobiography.

Africa, The Unknown Continent

North Africa was the only part of Africa the Europeans knew. And, of North Africa, they knew only the lands that touched the Mediterranean Sea. Those lands were rich in history. Egypt had once seen a civilization that produced pharaohs, pyramids, and a sphinx. That was more than 2,000 years before the birth of Christ. Much later, in the 9th century C.E., another great civilization flourished in North Africa. It was Islamic (also called "Muslim"), and it began in Arabia and spread to Morocco and Spain and Mediterranean Europe.

But what of the rest of the huge African continent? What was it like? Europeans knew almost nothing of it—although there were wild rumors of rich kingdoms and of seven lost cities.

There was a barrier of sand that kept the Europeans from learning much: the vast Sahara desert. A few people were able to cross those blazing desert sands. They were African or Arab traders who traveled from oasis to oasis carrying gold and slaves from lands to the south. It was a very dangerous journey.

Why didn't the Europeans just sail down the African coast and discover for themselves where that gold was coming from? They wanted to, but until the 15th century they couldn't do it. You see, their boats were powered by men with oars. Those boats were fine in the calm Mediterranean, but they weren't safe in the rough Atlantic waters. It was not until the 15th century that Europeans developed sophisticated sailing technology that allowed them to build caravels that could sail into the wind.

Then they got up their courage and began going down the coast, farther and farther, until the Portuguese sailor Vasco da Gama rounded the tip of Africa in 1498 and went on to India. Now, perhaps, the Europeans could stop along the African coast and visit the rich grasslands and forests below the Sahara. They could—if the Africans would let them.

But the people who lived in Africa weren't anxious to have outsiders come and explore or settle. They welcomed the Europeans as traders with goods they could use, but that was all. The Europeans couldn't land, take over, and mine the continent's gold, as they did in America. The African warriors were too strong. The Africans let the Europeans build a few trading posts, but nothing more. Besides, there were African diseases that frightened the Europeans.

So the Europeans didn't learn much about the peoples and cultures of the African continent. For them, it remained mysterious. If they had been able to explore, they would have discovered as much vari-

These bronze sculptures were carved in Benin, the country in West Africa that Olaudah Equiano was kidnapped from.

ety in Africa as in Europe. There were sophisticated empires and primitive cultures. There were sculptures cast in bronze and gold and useful iron objects hammered by village blacksmiths and cotton that weavers turned into handsome fabrics.

On the west coast of Africa, near the continent's bulge, the three great kingdoms of Ghana, Mali, and Songhai rose and fell between the time of the Roman Empire and the settling of North

America. The ruler of Mali, Mansa Musa, was a Muslim who in 1324 took so much gold to Mecca (the center of the Muslim world) that the world price of gold tumbled. In the 15th century, Timbuktu, the leading city of Songhai, was renowned for its schools and wise men. A visitor wrote of the city's "great store of doctors, judges, priests, and other learned men that are bountifully maintained at the King's cost...and hither are brought diverse manuscripts or written books... which are sold for more money than any other merchandise."

But by the time the sailing ships were able to call at West African ports, it was trade alone that interested both peoples. The Europeans had guns, iron, cloth, kettles, and mirrors that were wanted in Africa. The Africans had workers—healthy, hardy people—who were wanted to grow crops and mine and settle the place the Europeans called a New World.

And so men and women would be traded into slavery by people, on both sides of the Atlantic, who didn't seem to worry about the consequences of their actions.

He will take a European name. It is Gustavus Vassa.

Many Africans are sent to Virginia, where they are traded for tobacco. Some are exchanged for sugar and molasses in the West Indies. Others are traded for rice in South Carolina. Then the ships head back to their home ports.

In Newport, Rhode Island, where we started this voyage, the sugar and molasses are turned into rum—and the triangle begins again. That is the way the terrible triangular trade works. Every colony is a part of it. English ships carry the greatest numbers of Africans into slavery.

In the colonies, laws are soon passed that attempt to take away the blacks' humanity. The Virginia Black Code says slaves are property—not people. New York law says runaway slaves caught 40 miles north of Albany—on the way to Canada and safety—are to be killed.

Remember when the first black people arrived as indentured servants at Jamestown? In 1725 about 75,000 blacks are living in the American colonies. By 1790 there are more than 10 times that number.

A Dutch tobacco trader from New Amsterdam. Notice the slaves unloading tobacco in the background, and the town of New Amsterdam rising in the far distance. Who do you think the female figure on the left is?

39 Four and Nine Make Thirteen

This man has been brought to debtors' prison by his creditors (the people he owes money to), to stay there until he finds a way to pay them.

Tomochichi, leader of a Creek town near Savannah, welcomed Oglethorpe.

If you've been counting, you know I've talked about 12 colonies. Can you name them? Cover the next sentence and see if you can.

Here they are: Massachusetts, New Hampshire, Connecticut, Rhode Island, New York, New Jersey, Pennsylvania, Delaware, Maryland, Virginia, North Carolina, and South Carolina.

Finally, like a tail at the end of a kite, along came the 13th colony. Do you know what it was named? Here's a clue: It was founded in 1732, when KING GEORGE II was on the throne of England. That wasn't hard: it was Georgia.

Georgia's beginning was noble, not because of birth or wealth, but because of a noble idea. Unfortunately the idea didn't work out. Still, it was inspiring.

James Oglethorpe, who planned Georgia, wanted to solve a terrible problem. People in England who couldn't pay their bills were thrown into debtors' prisons. Once they were in those jails—and they were awful places—they couldn't work or earn money, and so they had no way to pay their debts. If they were lucky, a relative or friend came up with the cash. Otherwise they just stayed there. Many died in prison.

Oglethorpe decided to found a colony where debtors could go instead of going to jail. He wanted to make it a place where people could lead ideal lives. So he had laws passed for Georgia that made drinking liquor and keeping slaves illegal. He wanted Georgians to live on small farms, and he wanted them to do their own farming. He brought experts from Europe to teach them how.

Debtors' prisons in England stuck around for more than a century after Oglethorpe. The author Charles Dickens used his writing skills to help get rid of them. When Charles was a boy, his father had been thrown in debtors' prison—so he knew just how dreadful it was. He described those prisons in some of his novels—such as *Little Dorrit* and *Our Mutual Friend*. Those are long books, but they tell wonderful stories.

In 1734 settlers began building the town of Savannah. The tent under the tall trees in front of the houses was James Oglethorpe's.

149

These Lutherans left Austria to find freedom to worship in Georgia. The verse says their only companion is the Gospel—having left their homeland, they are in God's hands.

Oglethorpe helped to plan a handsome capital, Savannah, a city with beautiful parks and fine public squares. It was a shame his idea didn't work out. Not many debtors wanted to come to the wilds of Georgia. To some, even prison seemed safer.

Those who came were much like the settlers in the other colonies: a mixture of peoples and religions. Anglican men and women came, German Lutherans came, Catholics came, Jews came, and so did Scotch Presbyterians.

They soon discovered that Georgia was full of Indian villages. When the first settlers arrived, they found thousands of Indian mounds. The mounds were sacred sites from the Native American past. (If you get into a helicopter and fly near Eatonton, Georgia, you can see one of those earth mounds. It is shaped like an eagle with wings that spread out for 120 feet, about the size of four average classrooms.)

The local Indians had bad memories of white people. Back in 1540, the Spanish conquistador Hernando de Soto had marched through Georgia with his army. De Soto was so cruel and evil that the Indians were still telling stories about him 200 years later.

But Oglethorpe was a fine and honorable man, and the Indians learned to trust him. They made many peace treaties with him and both he and they always kept their word.

It was the settlers who gave Oglethorpe problems. They wanted to drink liquor and have slaves, and eventually they won out. When Oglethorpe tried to force his laws and "good ideas" on others, it just didn't work.

Besides, life in Georgia wasn't easy. Spaniards and pirates gave the settlers a hard time. Pirates roamed along the Georgia coast, capturing ships of all nations. Spain controlled Florida and said Georgia and the Carolinas were also her territories. Because of that, there were constant border fights. When the Spaniards attacked, the Georgians were able to fight them off—luckily for them, because none of the other colonies helped out. It was a while before the colonies thought of uniting, or of helping each other.

James Edward Oglethorpe, founder of Georgia.

Oglethorpe lost all his money trying to establish Georgia. Finally, he gave up. Georgians wanted to have rice plantations and slaves and the king's government, and that is what they got. The king made Georgia into another royal colony (in 1752). That made eight royal colonies: Virginia, Massachusetts, New Hampshire, North Carolina, New York, South Carolina, New Jersey, and Georgia. Each had a royal governor, appointed by the king.

Rhode Island and Connecticut had charters that allowed them to govern themselves. Their assemblies (congresses) picked their governors. Maryland, Pennsylvania, and Delaware were proprietary colonies. They were owned by individuals—the Calverts and the Penns.

All the colonies had assemblies of local leaders who made most of their laws. Later England would regret the freedom she gave the colonies and try to take some of it back. That would lead to big trouble.

But in the mid-18th century most Americans were happy to be part of the mighty British empire. The 13 colonies were like 13 children of a kindly and faraway parent. Each colony seemed to be a tiny nation, with its own government, its own habits, and its own religious ways.

They were different—one from another—but in some ways they were all a bit like Europe. Each had a measure of European class society. So, if you really wanted to be independent, if you wanted to be the equal of anyone, the place to be was on the frontier. There, it was your intelligence and your strength that made you a leader. On the frontier no one cared if you were Puritan or Baptist. It didn't make a difference if your father was a lord or a pauper. Could you be depended upon? Did you tell the truth? Could you shoot straight? Were you brave? That's what mattered on the frontier.

The frontier offered something even more important: *land*. Land meant everything in a society that lived by farming. *Owning land made you feel really free.*

People were arriving in America every day. Much of the land on the East Coast was taken. The frontier was where these newest Americans were going. They were heading to the tree-thick mountains that bordered the coastal plains—and then on, over those mountains.

A famous English poet, Alexander Pope (he wrote that "A little learning is a dangerous thing"), composed a short verse, or couplet, about Oglethorpe (they were friends):
One driven by strong benevolence of soul,
Shall fly like Oglethorpe from pole to pole.
What does that mean?

James Oglethorpe (in black) brought some of his Indian friends to London. In this picture he is introducing them to the trustees of his new colony.

151

40 Over the Mountains

Look at the map of the 13 colonies on page 94 to see how the colonies hug the East Coast. You will also see the Appalachian mountains running all the way down the left boundary of the colonies, blocking the way west.

A family traveling west lights a fire. Imagine cooking dinner at night in the rain and the unknown.

Look at a map. Notice: all the early English-speaking settlements are on or near the East Coast. That's not surprising, since the settlers came by boat from Europe. Most of them stayed near the place they landed.

Yet, almost from the first, a few settlers wanted to know what the land was like to the west. They came back with tales that made others want to go, too. Some went because they thought they would find the Pacific Ocean; some went west to trade with the Indians; a few were criminals who were chased away from the settlements. Most didn't get far.

Look at the map again, and you'll see why. Do you see that long strip of mountains that runs from north to south and makes a spine down the back of the eastern United States? Those are the Appalachian Mountains, and they stretch from Quebec to Alabama.

The Appalachians are the oldest mountains in our country. They are tall, but not as tall as some of the far western mountains. The Appalachians have been rounded and smoothed by millions of years of wind and rain.

Don't be confused if you hear of White Mountains in New Hampshire, Green

The Swedish introduced log houses to the New World. They were just right for places that had a lot of trees and not much else.

Can you guess the remote location of this lonely log cabin, surrounded by thick forests? It's a few miles from Baltimore, Maryland. In the 18th century you didn't have to go far to be out in a wilderness.

Mountains in Vermont, Catskill Mountains in New York, Allegheny Mountains in Pennsylvania, and Blue Ridge, Clinch, Shenandoah, and Great Smoky Mountains in the South. All these mountains are part of the Appalachian range.

Water from Appalachian streams and snows flows in two directions. Some water goes into rivers that drain into the Atlantic; some goes to rivers that drain into the Gulf of Mexico. The spot high on the mountains where the waters change direction is called a "divide."

Have you ever climbed a mountain? It isn't easy—even today, when there are clear trails. Imagine what it was like for the first trailblazers. The pioneers who went into Vermont couldn't even take horses. They had to go on foot, because the mountains were so thick with trees that no grass could grow. So there was nothing for horses to eat. Those explorers had to go with their axes, cut down trees, plant seeds, and wait for a crop before they could bring animals.

The trailblazers were first, but they were soon followed by people looking for land to farm. Usually mountain land isn't easy to farm, so they didn't stay in the mountains. They went on, over the Appalachians, to the valleys or the flat lands beyond. There was no government where they went, so they were on their own. They had to fight Indians and other settlers for their land. They were a tough breed, those early over-the-mountain people. They had to be in order to survive.

Oh, Shenandoah

Alexander Spotswood, the Virginia governor we met earlier, was a big booster of westward expansion. In 1716 he set out with an expedition into Virginia's mountainous wilderness. They traveled 200 miles, named the Blue Ridge Mountains (a trick of the light makes them look blue), and got to the Shenandoah Valley. When they came home, Spotswood gave each expedition member a tiny gold horseshoe (because their horses had to be shod to manage the rocky mountain paths). They became known as the "Knights of the Golden Horseshoe."

Talleyrand, who was a French prince and one of the most important politicians in Europe in Napoleanic times. He is supposed to have said: "The United States has 32 religions but only one dish." He didn't think much of Yankee cooking.

Do you use the expression "I'm stumped" when you're stuck about what to do or think? In the days when westbound wagons traveled terrible roads like this one—where tree stumps stuck out of the ground—if you hit a stump, you were in trouble: "stumped."

Most didn't have time to write of their adventures, so we have to listen to others to try and understand what it must have been like. A famous French diplomat named Talleyrand visited the United States at the end of the 18th century. He wrote of a trip west. Talleyrand had a guide, and he went on horseback. This is what he saw:

I was struck with astonishment; less than 154 miles away from the capital [Philadelphia] all trace of men's presence disappeared. Nature, in all her primeval vigor, confronted us. Forests as old as the world itself...here and there the traces of former tornadoes that had carried everything before them. Enormous trees, all mowed down in the same direction, extending for a considerable distance, bear witness to the wonderful force of these terrible phenomena....To be riding through a large wild forest, to lose one's way in it in the middle of the night, and to call to one's companion in order to ascertain that you are not missing each other; all this gives impressions impossible to define....When I cried, "...are you here?" and my companion replied, "Unfortunately I am, my lord," I could not help laughing at our position.

41 Westward Ho

Daniel Boone was a "long hunter," so called because he stayed in the wilderness for weeks.

The British tried to stop them. They didn't want settlers moving west. The British were in charge, and that meant they had to keep order. If the settlers moved into Indian territory, someone had to worry about protecting them from Indian attack. Someone had to protect the Indians from rifle-happy settlers. Someone had to make treaties with the Indians and do some governing.

That cost money. Britain would have to build forts in the western territories. She would have to send soldiers to man those forts. She would have to send governors. Parliament told the colonists to stay out of Indian territory.

But there was no stopping them. Some people want to go where no one has gone before. Some people are born explorers. Some people are just restless. The Americans who headed for the frontiers were all of those things—and more.

They were people who were looking for a good life, and they hadn't found it on the East Coast. By the middle of the 18th century the best land in the East was taken, and society was already in place. These people weren't content to sit around and be second-best. They were the kind who would sail across a dangerous ocean to try their luck in a new world. That kind of person was willing to risk everything for adventure or the dream of a better life.

So they headed out—and you had to be brave to do that—into the unknown wilds. They were called frontiersmen and frontierswomen, trailblazers and pathfinders. They lived in the woods, shot the food they ate, and made their own clothes. They learned from the Indians and from each other. One of them was a man named Daniel Boone.

Daniel Boone was born in 1734, two years after James Oglethorpe

Do you know why "buck" is another word for *dollar*? It's because in the days of Daniel Boone and the Long Hunters, a buckskin was worth about a dollar—so the money was named for the deer that it bought.

Daniel was not the first Boone to seek adventure. His ancestors were Normans—soldiers and farmers from French Normandy—who conquered England in the 11th century and settled there because of the good land and opportunity. To them, then, England seemed a frontier on the edge of the world.

Women and children from settler families were sometimes kidnapped by Indians during border battles over territory. Daniel Boone's own daughter, Jemima, was carried off in 1776, but he managed to rescue her. This is an artist's rather romantic idea of the event.

Have you ever seen a picture of Daniel Boone in a coonskin cap? Well, those pictures were drawn by people who didn't know Boone. He wore a broad-brimmed hat to protect his eyes from the sun.

founded Georgia. Oglethorpe would have liked Daniel Boone, and John Smith would have like him, too. Daniel Boone didn't look for others to do his work. He grew up in Pennsylvania, with Indians for friends, and he learned their ways along with the ways of the European settlers. That was an interesting combination, and it was creating a new people, a people who were wholly American.

Daniel Boone's grandfather, George Boone, had lived in England, where he was a weaver and an independent thinker. He was both cautious and daring, a man who would do what he intended and do it well. When he was 36 years old George Boone left the Church of England and joined an outcast religion that some people called Quaker. Boone knew it as the Society of Friends.

Being a Quaker in England was hard, as we've already seen. Quakers were persecuted, but George Boone stood up for his beliefs.

Then he heard about William Penn's colony in America, where Quakers and everyone had equal rights. He also heard stories of abundant land cheap enough for anyone to buy, and that seemed almost too good to be true.

As I said, Boone was cautious. He had a wife and nine children. Before he moved his whole family, he sent his three oldest children to the New World to look around. This was what George Boone learned in a letter from Pennsylvania:

> Because one may hold as much property as one wishes and pay when one wishes, everybody hurries to take up property. The farther the Germans and English cultivate the country the farther the Indians retreat. They are agreeable and peaceable....in summer one can shoot a deer, dress the skin, and wear pants from it in twenty-four hours.

It sounded good to him. In 1717, when he was 51 years old—an old man in those days—George Boone left England and sailed for Pennsylvania. Boone's grandson, Daniel, became the most famous of all the American frontiersmen.

Daniel Boone's first adventures came in 1755, during the French and Indian War (which you'll read more about in Book 3). He fought on the side of the British, as did George Washington. Washington was an officer; Boone was a wagon driver. Sitting with soldiers around the campfire, young Boone heard John Finley, a fur trader, tell stories of a land the Indians called *kentake*, which means "meadow-land." Finley said it was the most beautiful land he had ever seen, filled with high grasses, birds, buffalo, deer, and beaver. It was an Indian hunting ground, and the Indians didn't want the white men to find it.

Daniel Boone got excited about those meadowlands over the mountains. As soon as the war was over, off he went, with a sack of salt around his neck, an ax in his belt, and a rifle over his shoulder. But he never found an easy way to get over the mountains.

Then, one day, a peddler knocked on his door. It turned out to be John Finley. Finley told him of an Indian trail through the mountains.

Boone searched until he found that trail. It led to a hole through the mountains, called a gap, and that led to the rich grasslands of Kentucky. In 1775 Daniel Boone and 30 woodsmen turned that Indian trail into a road that families could travel with wagons and animals. It was called the "Wilderness Road," and it went for 300 miles. By 1790, almost 200,000 people had gone west on the Wilderness Road.

Three years after Daniel Boone first reached Kentucky, settlers were already pouring in. A man named James Harrod was laying out a town named after him. Pretty soon there was a town named after Boone, too—Boonesborough.

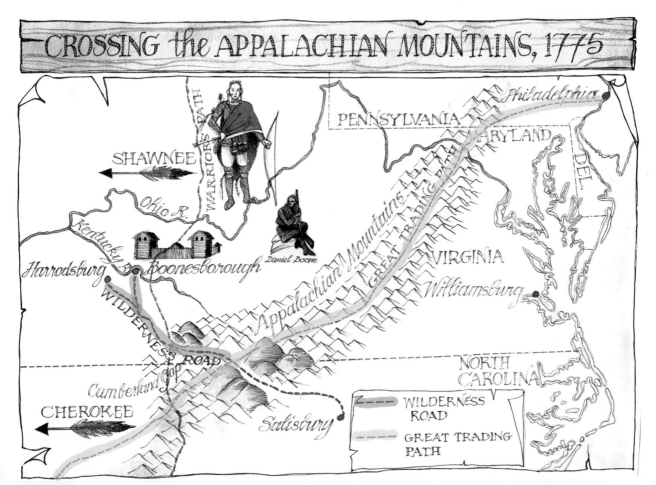

CROSSING the APPALACHIAN MOUNTAINS, 1775

SHAWNEE

WARRIOR'S PATH

Ohio R.

Daniel Boone

Kentucky R.

Harrodsburg

Boonesborough

PENNSYLVANIA

Philadelphia

MARYLAND

DEL.

Appalachian Mountains

GREAT TRADING PATH

VIRGINIA

Williamsburg

WILDERNESS ROAD

Cumberland Gap

CHEROKEE

Salisbury

NORTH CAROLINA

WILDERNESS ROAD

GREAT TRADING PATH

This bloody picture of *An Attack of the Indians upon Dan'l and Squire Boone & John Stewart* helped spread the legends told about Boone after his death. (Squire Boone was Daniel's brother.)

But Daniel Boone just couldn't stay settled. He was always off on one adventure or another. The Indians didn't want Boone or any whites in Kentucky. Then they hoped the settlers would at least all stay in one place. They soon learned that there was no way to keep Daniel Boone from wandering. He was a natural-born explorer, and, like a cat, he had nine (or maybe more) lives. His wife was told he was dead—more than once—and a few times he was close to it, but he always survived, whether his attackers were animals or people.

Sometimes he ran backward through the woods, and Indians following his trail went the wrong way. Once he swung 40 feet on a grapevine so Indians would lose his trail. The stories about Boone's adventures grew and grew and grew, and some of them were true: stories about how he was captured by Indians, about how he rescued his daughter from Indians, about a buffalo stampede, about how he was adopted into a tribe. Each time the stories got told, they were bigger and better.

It was said that Daniel Boone could shoot a flea off the nose of a bear. Do you think that could be true?

We would know for sure if it weren't for a canoe accident. When Daniel was an old man, he told his grandson about his adventures. His grandson wrote them all down in a book. Everyone who knew Daniel Boone agreed that he was honest, so that book must have told the real story about him. But the book was in a canoe when the Boone family moved; the canoe tipped; and the book was lost.

We do know for sure that when Daniel was a boy one of his best friends was named Abraham Lincoln. Many years later, that Abraham's grandson became a famous president. President Lincoln was proud that his grandfather had known Daniel Boone, because Daniel Boone was a real American hero.

42 The End—and the Beginning

Congratulations! You have finished almost all of book 2 of *A History of US*. The 13 colonies have been formed, and are doing very well!

We have traveled into the 18th century, and those early days of hunger and hardship are now only a memory. Life is beginning to be comfortable for the settlers in this New World. It still takes courage to cross the dangerous Atlantic and begin again on a continent that is reshaping itself. But, just as the birth of a baby offers promise and hope, so, too, this vast, inviting land promises hope to all who are tired of the Old World ways.

Many people have come to America because there was no opportunity for them in that Old World. Most of those people think they have found paradise in this land of sweet-smelling flowers, abundant game, and fertile soil. In England, men are shot for hunting the king's deer. In America, deer, beaver, birds, and fish are for everyone.

Some of those who are here have a powerful dream of a free country where everyone is treated fairly. The dreamers will have the opportunity to test their ideas. They will turn 13 colonies into a nation "conceived in liberty, and dedicated to the proposition that all men are created equal."

If you keep reading our history, you will learn about the making of that nation—our nation. You will meet people like George Washington and Thomas Jefferson. You will learn more about Benjamin Franklin and Daniel Boone. The story will include war, adventure, heroism, villainy, and love. So keep on reading America's story. There is much excitement ahead.

This painting of George Washington was made when he was a young colonel in the Virginia militia—at the very beginning of what was to be an extraordinary career.

After Words: A Cartographer Makes Maps, Not Wagons

*C*artography. (car TOG ruf fee) No, it doesn't have anything to do with wagons. It is the art of making maps. It comes from Latin roots: *carta*, or *charta,* meaning paper, especially paper made from papyrus, and *graphie*, from the Greek word for "writing."

Just look out the window and you'll see: the world is flat. And yet the ancient Greeks four thousand years ago, realized that the world is a sphere. (If you have any doubts about it, we now have photographs taken in space that show our beautiful green and blue globe.) The Greeks didn't have telescopes or fancy measuring devices. How did they figure out the shape of the Earth? They used their brains.

The oldest collection of maps still in existence today is a Song work from China which dates, we think, to 1099. It has 44 maps and was printed from woodblocks by a mapmaker named Shui Anli.

This original Coronelli globe, which dates from 1688, is on permanent display in the Texas Tech University Library in Lubbock, Texas.

Father Vincenzo Coronelli (vin CHEN zo CORE oh NELLY), who lived in the Republic of Venice in Italy, knew as much about the world as any person in the 17th century. (It was the century of Peter Stuyvesant, William Penn, and most of the people in this book.) That may seem surprising, because he was a Franciscan monk – a member of an order of priests (founded by Saint Francis of Assisi) who agree to a life of poverty when they join that religious order. But the Franciscans are also scholars, and Father Coronelli was among the best of them..

He spent much of his life doing one of the most important tasks of his time, or any time: making maps.

Mapmaking doesn't sound significant to you? Well, hold on, I'll try and convince you that it is.

What is a map and why is it important? Maps are sources of information. They are guides. They are usually drawings of something too big to see with a sweep of your eyes. They are a way of simplifying things too complicated to hold in your head easily. Sometimes they help you look to the future. Some people even map ideas.

The simplest maps get you from here to there. Find yourself in a new city and it helps to have a map that will guide you. That will save you time, aggravation, or maybe even disaster. Suppose you're going to a foreign land, or you're a merchant sending goods far away, or perhaps you are commanding an army on its way to battle. Imagine that you have no map of your route or your destination. What will you pay for one? And what about the rest of the world? Do you know where you are in relation to other places?

In medieval times world maps were usually disc shaped, looking like a coin, but bigger. On most European maps, Jerusalem and the Mediterranean Sea were in the center, and Asia, Africa, and Europe surrounded them. On Japanese maps, Japan was in the center. On Korean maps, Korea was in the center. You get the idea. Maps are human creations, and we all like to think of our culture as central.

After Columbus returned from his voyage, and especially after Magellan's ship made it around the globe, Europe's view of the world was stretched. Suddenly there were new worlds to know. Lots of Europeans wanted to explore, or conquer, or invest, or exploit. Picture the excitement of the times. And the greed. The nations that won the exploration game were going to dominate the globe. But you can't explore without maps. Mapmakers, who were now in big demand and short supply, became very important people.

The best European maps of the time were based on those of the ancient Greek geographer, Ptolemy (who lived in the 2nd century C.E.), and on maps by Arabs (like the 12th-century scholar Al-Idrisi). In the 15th century, Portuguese sailors began bringing new information home. Their maps, which they treated like secret documents, were soon among the most precise in the world.

To make maps you have to be smart. Accurate maps are drawn to scale. That means a millimeter or an inch on the map needs to reflect exactly the meters or feet or miles in the real world. So mapmakers need to know mathematics. They have to be able to draw. They need to understand landforms, like mountains and valleys. They need to be aware of the latest scientific findings. The country with the best mapmakers usually has the most power and prestige. (Is it different today? What new territories are we now mapping? Who is doing it?)

How do you make a flat map of a round globe? Explorers need flat maps. They need to be able to follow a straight line from point A to point B. To understand the problem, take an orange peel. Now try and make a flat map of that peel. You can't do it. There will be tears and irregularities. There's no way to chart a direct line from one

Now when I was a little chap I had a passion for maps. I would look for hours at South America, or Africa, or Australia, and lose myself in all the glories of exploration. At that time there were many blank spaces on the earth, and when I saw one that looked particularly inviting on a map (but they all look like that) I would put my finger on it and say, *When I grow up I will go there. . .*
From *Heart of Darkness*, by Joseph Conrad

Al-Idrisi, who was born in Morocco about 1100, drew this map of the world. Can you locate the Mediterranean Sea?

When Columbus returned from his voyage in 1493 it changed the way Europeans thought of the world. This is the first map we have that reflects that new world view and includes the Americas. The mapmaker, Giovanni Contarini, signed his name and the date, 1506. That's all we know of him. Like Columbus, Contarini thought that Asia was just beyond the New World islands. He has Brazil reach to the South Pole.

Abraham Ortelius, a 16th century Belgian, is remembered as the first cartographer to draw world maps in a uniform size, bind them together, and make an atlas. This famous map of his was published about 70 years after Columbus's voyage. It reflects a belief in a vast southern continent, Terra Australias.

Knowing latitude is easy, longitude is not. A very good book by Dava Sobel, *Longitude*, tells an exciting story of the big prize offered in the 18th century for a method to find longitude at sea.

part of the skin around the whole thing after you've flattened it. So you have to look for a next-best solution.

In 1569 Gerhardus Mercator (GAIR har dus mer KATE er), who lived in Flanders (now parts of Belgium, France, and the Netherlands), came up with an idea. He put a stiff piece of paper around a globe. Picture the paper as a cylinder with the round Earth inside. Then Mercator projected the Earth's three-dimensional shape onto the two-dimensional paper. That projection worked fine for the areas close to the equator. But think of your orange peel flattened. In the center it's okay, but near the poles it's a torn, ragged mess. Mercator didn't want tears or gaps on his maps. He wanted to be able to draw straight lines from one place to another. So he filled in the tears and gaps by stretching the regions to the north and south, making them bigger than they actually are.

As soon as he did that he could draw straight lines of latitude and longitude on his map. That was very helpful to sailors who could look at his maps and see hazards to avoid or havens to seek. Then, if they could figure out their own longitude and latitude, they could know exactly where they were on the map.

Mercator was a poor boy whose good mind and hard-working habits took him far. He often went without sleep to study mathematics, geography, astronomy, and surveying. By the time he was 24 he was a well-known engraver and maker of scientific instruments. When he died, at 82 in 1594, he had revolutionized mapmaking and gone into the history books as one of the best mapmakers of all time. (His neighbors praised him as a modest good citizen who often helped the poor.) His maps were not only the latest scientific records of world geography, they were superb pieces of art. People everywhere wanted his maps; and the best mapmakers—like John

Smith—were soon copying his methods. Most maps that you see are still based on the Mercator projection.

But keep in mind, it has a big flaw. Those stretched spaces distort the real space. Greenland, for instance, because it is near the North Pole, has to be huge on Mercator's map. Much, much bigger than Australia or South America. The truth is, it is actually much, much smaller than either of those places. There is no way to make a flat map that is an accurate picture of a globe. On page 166 you will see several approaches to the problem.

Now, finally, back to Father Vincenzo Coronelli. He lived a century after Mercator and he created some of the most gorgeous maps and globes of his time, or any time. Many of the people in this book must have known of Coronelli's maps. He built a globe for King Louis XIV of France that was 13' in diameter (think of two tall men head to head and toe to toe straddling a globe). It was the largest globe that had ever been built, and was a wonder of the time.

Coronelli, like the other Franciscans, dressed in a brown robe with a rope belt and wore sandals on his feet, but he hobnobbed with Europe's monarchs. That worked well for him and for them. In addition to supporting his work, they sent him the latest information on their conquests and explorations. It made his maps the best there were.

Coronelli put most of Australia on his globe, before anyone else did, and he filled in the interior of the other continents with rivers and bays that had rarely been marked before. He showed the St. Lawrence, the Yangtzee, the Senegal, the Paraguay, and the Zambezi rivers (which are where?). He included details on the latest exploration of the Mississippi River. And he made a special map of Siam (Thailand) based on an expedition of Jesuit Fathers sent by King Louis XIV. When he drew the seas, he added pictures of the

This gorgeous map of the Caribbean Sea and the West Indies was drawn about 1547. That finger pointing upwards from the bottom center is Florida. Mexico City is upper left. Is something wrong? Not at all. We expect North to be on top and South on the bottom. But they don't have to be that way. Turn the page around and you'll see Florida in its familiar place.

This map, printed in 1687, was color coded to mark European land claims. (No one considered Native American claims.) The mapmaker, Giovanni de Rossi, drew California as an island, So did others of his time. Rossi was pro-French. He gave everything colored pink to France.

In 1688 Father Vincenzo Coronelli, working in Venice, Italy (using information sent by Catholic Jesuit priests), made this map (*right*) of the Great Lakes (then a barely explored region of western New France). Compare it with today's satellite photograph of the same area (*below*). Amazing, isn't it?

164

wooden ships that were bringing Europeans so much astounding new information. His maps were works of art.

In 1684, Coronelli founded the world's first geographic society: the Cosmographic Academy of the Argonauts. If you joined (it was expensive) you got world map sheets, piece by piece, as they were produced. Then you could put them together to make a globe. Sometimes you got pages of a great atlas. (It was Mercator who coined that word "atlas" for a book of maps.) The king of Poland was one of Father Coronelli's subscribers. In 1688 Coronelli put himself in a corner of a great globe he made. (I know globes don't have corners, but when the globe is flattened onto a two-dimensional page, you get corners.)

Venice, like Portugal and Spain, had been a center of world power, but Coronelli could sense the shift that was in progress. France, the Netherlands, and now England were expanding their reach—all were producing great explorers and great mapmakers; they went hand in hand.

In the late 16th century, European surveyors began using a mathematical principle, *triangulation*. If you know the length of the base of a triangle and the size of its two angles you can figure out the size of the whole triangle. This 1594 German engraving shows surveyors at work.

In Greek mythology, the Argonauts were heroes who sailed on the ship *Argo* with Jason in search of the Golden Fleece.

About Maps and the Truth

Maps lie. All of them. You just can't tell the whole truth on a flat map. When you project that three-dimensional globe onto a flat two-dimensional page, you are forced to distort. There is no way around it. Still, maps are very important and useful. And, as long as you know about distortions, you can allow for them. We've developed many kinds of projections —some do one thing, some another. No one is perfect. The important thing is to choose the right projection for your needs. The best map services, like USGS (U.S. Geological Survey) use different projections for different purposes. You can compare the projections below.

For mariners, Mercator's projection (A) used to work best. It helped bring about the Age of Exploration. Mercator knew a grid would give sailors straight lines to follow. On the globe, lines of latitude come together. To make his grid work and keep latitude lines parallel, he had to flatten the globe and stretch land and sea, especially near the polar regions. (Note Greenland, which is actually about one eighth the size of South America.) Mercator projections are still widely used.

In 1963 Arthur Robinson developed a projection (B) that is now widely used in classrooms. Although it has some distortions (check Greenland again), mostly it shows the world's land as it actu-

ally looks. Robinson turned the whole globe into a one-sided elongated ellipse (or flattened oval), so his is called an elliptical projection. The world map near the end of this book is based on a Robinson projection. It is a very useful compromise. I like it.

Maps can sometimes give you wrong ideas about geographical importance. In the 1970s, Arno Peters, a German historian, said the Mercator projection glorified Europe and North America by making them large and on top, thus diminishing the Third World. (Check Africa on Peters' projection (C). His projection gives landmasses their true size (but it distorts shape). The Peters projection is often shown with South on top, as below.

Most of the standard projections are made by putting a cylinder around a globe and projecting the globe's image on it. A conic projection (D) is made with a cone placed over a region of the Earth. You need several conic projections to capture the whole Earth.

Global gores (E) are tapered strips that, put together, make a globe. They are highly accurate, but not easy to use. You can see why.

You can get more information on maps from the USGS website, www.usgs.gov, or by calling 1-888-ASK-USGS. USGS, a government agency, belongs to you and all citizens.

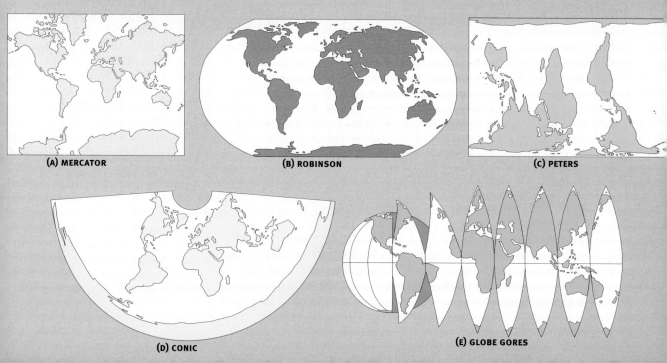

(A) MERCATOR **(B) ROBINSON** **(C) PETERS**

(D) CONIC **(E) GLOBE GORES**

Some Measuring Words

Acre. (AYE kur) It's a unit of measurement used in the U.S. An acre is an area of land or sea equal to 43,560 square feet. It used to be what a yoke of oxen could plow in one day. (What's a yoke of oxen?)

Cubit. (KEW bit) In the Bible, when God gave Noah the measurements of the ark, he used cubits. For a long time, lots of people measured in cubits. It was supposed to be the distance between the elbow and the tip of the middle finger. Today a cubit is 18 inches or 45.72 cm., but the measurement is mostly a historic thing. The Latin word for "elbow" is cubitum.

Knot. Yes, it is what you get in a rope or in your hair if you aren't neat. The word actually has a number of meanings (check your dictionary). But the meaning that has to do with measuring is used by sailors. It is a measure of the speed of a ship. A knot is one nautical mile per hour (or 1,85 kilometers per hour).

League. It's a collection of baseball teams. It's also 3 miles or 4.8 kilometers. In the 17th and 18th centuries people often measured in leagues. They don't do that much today.

Light year. It is the distance that light travels in a vacuum in one year. That's about 5.88 trillion miles or 9.46 trillion kilometers. For measuring purposes you can consider space a vacuum. So if a star is 600 light years away, how far is it?

There are many other measuring words, some used today, some archaic (ar KAY ick, it means out of date). See if you can find some. (Helpful hint: check your dictionary for a measurement table.)

WORDS ABOUT THINGS (MOSTLY IMAGINARY) USEFUL TO UNDERSTAND MAPS

Equator. An imaginary line around the middle of the earth.

Latitude. A measure of distance north and south of the equator. Latitude lines run east and west around the globe and are parallel to each other. They are measured in degrees, minutes, and seconds. There are 90 degrees of north latitude and 90 degrees of south latitude. Each degree of latitude and longitude is divided into 60 minutes (60'), and minutes into 60 seconds (60").

Prime Meridian. An imaginary line running north-south and right through Greenwich, England. The prime meridian is 0°.

Longitude. The distance, measured in degrees, east or west of the prime meridian. There are 180 degrees of west longitude and 180 degrees of east longitude. Longitude lines meet at the poles. They are not parallels.

International Date Line. An imaginary line running north-south through the Pacific Ocean, mostly along the 180th meridian. There, by international agreement, travelers change dates. Going westward one adds a day, going eastward means going back in time.

Scale. A small distance on a map represents a larger distance in the real world. Scale is the ratio of map size to actual size. Example: one half-inch on a map may represent one foot of land.

Coordinates. The numbers that tell a place's exact longitude and latitude are called its coordinates. The coordinates of Washington, D.C. are 38.54° North (latitude) and 77.2° West (longitude).

Isothermal. This word has to do with temperature. You'll find isotherm lines, showing temperatures, on climate maps.

Geology, A Storyteller's Science

Maps are snapshots of Earth at a given time. But Earth's face keeps changing. Earthquakes, volcanoes, erosion, climate, and glaciers help create that change. So do the huge tectonic plates that hold up the continents and oceans. New sea floor is constantly being formed and that pulls and tugs on the tectonic plates. Most of the United States (except the west coast and Hawaii) lies on the North American plate. The plates move along with the land that sits on them. Geological maps can help picture that activity. They add a fourth dimension — time — to cartography. One way geological maps picture time is by using different colors to show the varying ages of Earth's rock.

Here are some tidbits of U.S. geological history. How would you map them?

• The Rocky Mountains are youngsters, as mountains go (they are between 50 and 100 million years old), except for Pikes Peak—where you can find billion-year-old granite.

• Florida is an add-on to the United States. It was part of Africa until it floated our way.

• In central New York, Ice Age glaciers scoured valleys and then, when the glaciers melted, some of those valleys filled with water creating seven big Finger Lakes. (The Iroquois once believed that the fan-shaped lakes were marks from the hand of the Great Spirit.)

• Yellowstone National Park, in northwest Wyoming, lies above a hot spot or plume rising through Earth's crust from deep in the underlying mantle. Its hot springs (including Old Faithful) are souvenirs from an ancient volcano.

• The upper Rio Grande River flows south through New Mexico along a fault, the Rio Grande Rift, where lava from deep inside Earth periodically rises to the surface. Predictions are that a few million years from now, an ocean basin may spread across this area.

• About 20 million years ago, in the region that stretches from southern Oregon to western Texas, Earth's crust thinned, stretched, and broke into some 400 mountains creating the unique and often spectacular Basin and Range Region. Earth has many stories to tell. If you study geology you will learn about them.

Relief maps show the shape of the land's surface by using dark and light shadings. Leonardo da Vinci developed this technique in his drawings some 400 years ago. Artists call it *chiaroscuro* (key air oh SKYUR oh). Computers do it digitally. A computer (GIS) map can show terrain in relief across the world—a photograph is limited in its scope.

Meteorology is the study of weather and weather forecasting. Everyone knows about Ben Franklin and the lightning rod. But Ben was fascinated with the nature of weather and storms and did serious research in the field. He kept detailed records comparing wind and weather in several regions. (Imagine how excited he would be with today's satellite information gathering.)

Geologists have devised this computer-generated map showing the age of the rock that makes up the continental United States. The colors yellow to green indicate rock formed from 1 to 245 million years ago. The blue to purple shades indicate rock from 246 to 438 million years ago, and the darkening shades of red indicate rock from 449 to 2600 millions years ago.

Being Up to Date

Way back in time, when we didn't know much about the world, mapmaking was a form of artistry and maps were often gorgeous works that only the elite could afford. Then, as we explored unknown areas, more and more maps got drawn. You couldn't develop land, or settle on it, if you didn't know where you were. Accurate maps were in demand. Usually there was no time to be artistic.

Early in the 20th century, photographers climbed into airplanes and began taking aerial photographs of the land. Those photographs were not maps, but they helped make ever-more accurate maps. So did satellites when they were fired into the atmosphere, sending back stunning and precise earth portraits. Landsat 1 was the first satellite with eyes for global mapping. A single Landsat 1 scene (115 miles by 115 miles) included more than thirty million observations. Each scene took 25 seconds to complete. Landsat 1, launched in 1972, was followed by ever-more sophisticated satellites. The total amount of information sent by Landsat satellites was, and is, staggering.

But, astonishing as satellite photography is, it doesn't tell the whole story. A whole new level of cartography came along when computers entered the field. Mountains of information can be processed in a computer, making for an incredible variety of maps. Computer-based mapping is known as GIS: it stands for Geographic Information Systems. GIS maps usually have a scale of 1:1,000,000 or better. That means we can now map tiny bits of land along with vast areas of space.

Computer mapping can show earthquakes throughout history, current fault lines, weather (past and present), temperature, population. . . the possibilities are endless. Computers keyed to satellites can locate you and your vehicle wherever you are and chart a route to your destination.

Cameras sometimes distort space; computers can make corrections. Computers have done something no one expected. They have helped make maps gorgeous again. Today, cartography is a "hot" science. And you don't have to be elite to have access to great maps. Just start on the Internet with the U.S.Geological Survey maps at **http://www.usgs.gov/research/gis/title.html**.

On August 10, 2001, a member of the crew of the Space Shuttle Discovery took this picture of a satellite circling the earth.

Isaac Newton's laws of motion predict the orbits of human-made satellites. The law of gravity tells us that force changes with distance from the Earth. Knowing that lets you figure out what accelerations to expect at different altitudes. Physicist Gerry Wheeler says, "a satellite at a height of 200 kilometers should orbit the Earth in 88.5 minutes. This is close to the orbit of the satellite Vostok 6 that carried the first woman, Valentina Tereskova, into Earth orbit in June 1963."

Chronology of Events

WARNING: CHRONOLOGIES CAN BE DANGEROUS!

Medical reports tell of a disease—called *date-itis*—with these alarming symptoms: rapid heartbeat, heavy sweating, and frequent moaning. This disease is caused by an allergy to dates. Teachers need to be aware that this has nothing to do with dried fruit! This not-very-rare disease affects people who hate to memorize dates. If the disease is treated skillfully, recovery is possible.

NOTICE TO POSSIBLE VICTIMS OF THE DISEASE:

Before reading this page: place a glass of water in your hand, an ice pack on your head, and read rapidly. Chances are good that you will survive, and you might learn something, too.

1607: Three ships sent by the London Company land at Cape Henry, Virginia. Captain John Smith and others found Jamestown

1609: Henry Hudson sails up the Hudson River

1609–10: All but 60 of the 500 settlers in Jamestown die during the Starving Time

1610: Santa Fe founded in New Mexico

1612: Settlers plant tobacco in Virginia for the first time

1614: Pocahontas, daughter of Powhatan, marries John Rolfe in Jamestown

1619: The first African slaves arrive in Virginia, and the first representative government of the European colonies begins with Virginia's House of Burgesses

1620: The Pilgrims sail from England to Cape Cod on the *Mayflower*. They make a plan of government called the Mayflower Compact

1621: Massasoit, leader of the Wampanoag Indians, establishes peace with the Pilgrims

1622: Opechancanough leads a great massacre of English settlers around Jamestown

1626: The Dutch buy Manhattan Island from the Indians

1630–40: The Puritans keep arriving in New England and spreading through the Massachusetts Bay Colony and beyond

1632: Lord Calvert founds Maryland

1633: First school in the North American colonies founded in New Amsterdam

1636: Roger Williams founds Rhode Island; Thomas Hooker moves to Connecticut; Harvard College founded

1649: King Charles I of England is beheaded; Parliament rules

1660: Charles II restored to the English throne; Mary Dyer hanged in Massachusetts

1664: The British capture New Amsterdam and rename it New York

1665–66: London attacked first by the Great Plague and then by the Great Fire

1670: Charleston founded in South Carolina

1675–76: Massasoit's son Metacom fights New England's colonists in King Philip's War

1677: North Carolinians rebel against English taxes

1680: Pueblo Indians led by Popé attack the Spaniards and drive them out of Santa Fe

1681: William Penn founds Pennsylvania

1686: King James II sends Sir Edmund Andros to control New England colonists

1688: England's Glorious Revolution; James II deposed

1692: Witchcraft trials held in Salem, Massachusetts

1699: Williamsburg becomes capital of Virginia

1706: Birth of Benjamin Franklin in Boston

1732: James Oglethorpe founds Georgia

1734: Birth of Daniel Boone

1775: The Wilderness Road open to pioneers

More Books to Read

History and Biography

Aliki, *The Story of William Penn,* Prentice-Hall, 1964. This book is very easy to read and has colorful pictures.

Franklin Folsom, *Red Power on the Rio Grande,* Follett, 1973. The story of Popé and the Native American revolution of 1680.

Jean Fritz, *The Double Life of Pocahontas,* Putnam, 1983. Biography as it should be written: exciting and informative.

Jean Craighead George, *The First Thanksgiving,* Philomel, 1993. Just what it says: how the *Mayflower* colonists celebrated their first harvest.

Ann McGovern, *If You Lived in Colonial Times,* Scholastic, 1992. A clear, informative, colorful book. Part of a series that answers many questions about past times.

Marcia Sewall, *Thunder from the Sky,* Atheneum, 1995. What happens when the Pilgrims and the Wampanoags meet? Read this book and find out.

Historical Fiction

Patricia Clapp, *Constance: A Story of Early Plymouth,* Beech Tree Books, 1991. This is the imagined diary of a real girl, Constance Hopkins, the daughter of one of the original *Mayflower* Strangers. It's written (very well) by one of her descendants, and it is as lively and fun as Constance herself.

Rachel Field, *Calico Bush,* Macmillan, 1931. Marguerite Ledoux is a 13-year-old French orphan, bound out for six years to a family who move to the wilds of Maine in 1743. This story, written over 60 years ago, is real, fresh, and exciting. It might even make you cry.

Paul Fleischman, *Saturnalia,* HarperCollins, 1990. Fourteen-year-old William is a printer's apprentice in 1681 Boston—but he's also a captured Narraganset Indian trying to find a link with his past. This story is very well written and researched—and quite thrilling.

Sally M. Keehn, *I Am Regina,* Dell, 1991. This is based on a true story about an 11-year-old girl who was kidnapped by Indians in 1755 and lived with them for nine years before being returned to her mother and their home in western Pennsylvania.

Ann Petry, *Tituba of Salem Village,* Harper & Row, 1964. Tituba, a slave from Barbados, is sold to a minister who moves to Salem, Massachusetts. This thoughtful book tells the story of the Salem witchcraft trials from Tituba's imagined point of view.

Elizabeth George Speare, *The Sign of the Beaver,* Houghton Mifflin, 1983. Matt is alone in the woods in Maine while his father fetches his mother and sister. He's befriended by an Indian boy, Attean—and both boys learn some surprising things about each other.

Elizabeth George Speare, *The Witch of Blackbird Pond,* Dell, 1958. Seventeenth-century Connecticut is the setting for this classic tale of suspense and romance. Highly recommended.

Elizabeth Yates, *Amos Fortune: Free Man,* Dutton, 1950. Born a prince in 1710 in Africa, At-mun is captured, sold in Massachusetts, and, as Amos Fortune, works in slavery until he buys his freedom at the age of 60. He dies a respected free man in New Hampshire, aged about 90. A splendid and true story.

Poems, Folktales, a Play, Songs, and Food!

Suzanne I. Barchers and Patricia C. Marden, *Cooking Up U.S. History: Recipes and Research to Share with Children,* Teacher Ideas Press, 1991. Recipes and information about American food. You can learn how to make hasty pudding, berry ink, hardtack, snickerdoodles, gumbo, and sopapillas.

Arthur Miller, *The Crucible,* Viking, 1953. This is a play about the Salem witchcraft trials by a famous playwright. It is not hard to read.

Scott R. Sanders, *Hear the Wind Blow: American Folk Songs Retold,* Bradbury, 1985. I love this kind of book. Stories and songs and explanations.

Alvin Schwartz, *Scary Stories to Tell in the Dark: Collected from American Folklore,* Lippincott/ HarperCollins, 1981. Just what the title says.

Picture Credits

LOC: Library of Congress

NYPL: New York Public Library

Cover: Edward Hicks, Penn's Treaty with the Indians (detail), Gilcrease Museum, Tulsa; 5: The Granger Collection; 6–7: LOC; 8 (bottom): National Portrait Gallery, Smithsonian Institution / Art Resource; 9: Metropolitan Museum of Art, Harris Brisbane Dick Fund, 1959; 10 (bottom): Istitutuo Arti Grafiche, Bergamo; 10 (top), 11 (both): NYPL, Picture Collection; 14, 15 (bottom right): LOC; 16: NYPL, Picture Collection; 18: LOC; 19: Brown University, John Carter Brown Library; 20 (top): From André Thevet, Les Singularitéz de la France Antarctique, autrement nommé Amérique, engraved by Silvanus, printed by Christopher Plantin, Antwerp; 20 (bottom): title page from The New Life of Virginea, printed by Felix Kyngston for William Welby, London, 1612; 21: LOC; 23: The Granger Collection; 25–26 (bottom): LOC; 26: Courtesy the Association for the Preservation of Virginia Antiquities; 28: Jamestown Rediscovery; 29: LOC; 30: NYPL, Special Collections; 31: NYPL, Map Division (97-7398); 33: NYPL, Special Collections; 35: National Portrait Gallery, Smithsonian Institution / Art Resource; 36: LOC; 37 (left), 38 (top): New-York Historical Society; 38 (bottom): LOC; 40 (top): NYPL, Picture Collection; 41 (bottom): LOC; 42: NYPL, Archives and Manuscripts; 44: NYPL, Archives and Manuscripts; 45 (top): Pilgrim Hall; 45 (bottom): Joe Flying Horse, "Around the Rez" The Lakota Times (now called Indian Country Today) September 1989; 46 (both), 47: LOC; 48–49: Pilgrim Hall; 51 (left): NYPL, Picture Collection; 51 (right): LOC; 52: Harper's Weekly, March 9, 1895; 54: LOC; 55 (left): The Book of Animals; 55 (right): NYPL, Picture Collection; 56 (bottom): LOC; 58: Corbis; 59: American Antiquarian Society; 60: Massachusetts Archives; 61: Bequest of Maxim Karolik, Museum of Fine Arts, Boston; 62: NYPL, Picture Collection; 63 (left): British Library; 63 (right): LOC; 64 (bottom left): Courtesy, Winterthur Museum; 64 (top): British Museum; 64 (bottom right), 65: LOC; 67: Historical Society of Pennsylvania; 68, 69 (bottom): LOC; 69 (top): © JOHN HOPF Photography; 70: NYPL, Picture Collection; 71: Pierpoint Morgan Library; 72: Plimouth Plantation; 74 (top): from Samuel Seyer, Memoirs Historical & Topographical of Bristol, NYPL; 74 (bottom), 75: LOC; 76 (top): NYPL, Picture Collection; 76 (bottom): from Matthew Hopkins, Discoverie of Witches, NYPL; 77: British Library; 78: Courtesy, Peabody Essex Museum, Salem, Massachusetts; 79 (top): Massachusetts Historical Society; 80, 81 (left): LOC; 83: NYPL, Maps Division; 84–86, 87 (top): LOC; 87 (bottom): Hartford Courant; 88, 90 (bottom): from Pablo Beaumont, Cronica de Mechoacan, NYPL, Rare Books and Manuscripts; 90 (top; neg. no. 133131), 91 (neg. no. 11409): courtesy, Museum of New Mexico; 92: LOC; 93: NYPL, Picture Collection; 95: LOC; 96 (top): New-York Historical Society; 96 (bottom): LOC; 97: (top): New Amsterdam, Prototype View, 1650–1653, J. Clarence Davies Collection, Museum of the City of New York; 97 (middle and bottom), 98, 101–102: LOC; 103: Radio Times Hulton Picture Library; 104: from H. D. Traill, Social England, NYPL; 105 (left): LOC; 105 (right): Gabriel Thomas, Pennsylvania and West New-Jersey, published by A. Baldwin, London 1698; 106 (top): NYPL, Picture Collection; 106 (bottom): LOC; 107: The Library Company of Philadelphia; 108: Edward Hicks, Penn's Treaty with the Indians, Gilcrease Museum, Tulsa; 109: NYPL, Picture Collection; 110 (center and bottom right): LOC; 110 (top right and bottom left): Historical Society of Pennsylvania; 110 (top left): NYPL, Rare Books and Manuscripts; 111: Courtesy of the Harvard Portrait Collection, Bequest of Dr. John Collins Warren, 1856; 112: from Holley, The Life of Mr. Benjamin Franklin, 1848, Benjamin Franklin Collection, Yale University Library; 114: LOC; 115 (top): NYPL, Maps Division; 115 (bottom): LOC; 116 (left top and below): NYPL, Picture Collection; 116 (right top): Baltimore Museum of Art; 116 (bottom) art resource; 117 (top): NYPL, Picture Collection; 117 (bottom): LOC; 119: American Antiquarian Society; 120 (top): Dementi / Foster Studios, Richmond, Virginia; 120 (left): NYPL, Picture Collection; 121 (top): NYPL; 121 (bottom right): Justus Engelhardt Kuhn, Eleanor Darnall, Maryland Historical Society, Baltimore; 122: LOC; 122 (below): Colonial Williamsburg Foundation; 124 (right): Embroidered Sampler made by Sarah Afflick, age 7, Philadelphia Pennsylvania, 1796, silk on cotton, Cooper-Hewitt Museum/Smithsonian Institution/Art Resource, NY, Bequest of the Estate of Emily Coe Stowell; 125: LOC; 126 (below): Colonial Williamsburg Foundation; 127: Courtesy, Muscarelle Museum of Art, College of William and Mary; 128, 129: Colonial Williamsburg Foundation; 130, 131 (top): LOC; 132: Abby Aldrich Rockefeller Folk Art Center, Williamsburg, Virginia; 133 (bottom): Charleston Yearbook, 1884; 134: Louis Manigault after George Roupell, Mr. Peter Manigault and His Friends, Gibbes Museum of Art / Carolina Art Association; 135 (top): Harper's Weekly, January 5, 1867; 135 (bottom): Courtesy of The Charleston Museum, Charleston, South Carolina; 136 (top): New-York Historical Society; 136 (bottom): from Johnson, The Lives of High-Waymen and Pirates, 1736, NYPL; 137 (top two): from Johnson, Historie der Engelsche Zee-roovers, 1725, Harvard College Library, Harry Elkins Widener Collection; 137 (bottom): from Johnson, History of Pirates, 1724, Harvard College Library, Harry Elkins Widener Collection; 138, 139 (top left): Beej's Pirate Image Archive; 139 (bottom and right): Photograph by Diane Hardy, Department of Cultural Resources, North Carolina Maritime Museum; 140: LOC; 141 (top): NYPL, Picture Collection; 141 (bottom): Hartford Courant; 142 (top): Schomburg Center for Research in Black Culture; 142 (bottom): NYPL; 143, 144: LOC; 147: NYPL, Picture Collection; 148: Nieu Amsterdam, NYPL, I. N. Phelps Stokes Collection; 149 (top right): Guildhall Library, London; 149, 150: LOC; 151: Courtesy, Winterthur Museum; 152 (top): Museum of Science and Industry, Chicago; 152 (bottom): Cincinnati Historical Society; 153: LOC; 154: George Tattersall, Highways and Byeways of the Forest, M. and M. Karolik Collection, Museum of Fine Arts, Boston; 155: NYPL, Picture Collection; 156, 158: LOC; 159: Washington / Curtis / Lee Collection, Washington and Lee University, Lexington, Virginia; 160: Yale University Libraries; 161: Bodeleian Library, Oxford University; 162 (top): British Library; 162 (bottom): The Granger Collection; 163: NYPL; 164 (top): The Granger Collection; 164 (middle): LOC; 164 (botom): NASA; 165: The Granger Collection; 168: USGS; 169: NASA

Index

A Note from the Author

Imagine that we are British colonists. Most of us agree on these things:

Some people are better than others.

Some people are meant to be slaves.

Some people have a God-given right to rule.

Women are inferior to men.

We don't even question these ideas. We've grown up with them. If we are African-American or Native American we are doing some questioning. But we, too, come from cultures where slavery is practiced.

So what happened? Why do we think differently today? We're not smarter. What makes us see the world through a different prism?

I believe the answer is modern science. It opened minds. Even nonscientists began thinking in new ways.

Before 1550 there wasn't much science in the European world and its provinces. Everyone believed the earth stood still in the middle of the universe and the sun and stars moved around it. Earthquakes and lightning and tornadoes were acts of God, or the devil, and beyond human understanding.

Then, in rat-a-tat progression, along came Copernicus (ko-PUR-nih-kuss), Galileo (gal-ih-LAY-oh), Kepler, and Newton—who used their minds to search for answers to nature's puzzles. They discovered the universe has rules, and people can understand those rules.

Copernicus, Galileo, and Kepler were astronomers (worth reading about). They moved the sun into center field and set the earth orbiting around it. It wasn't an easy job. The old-style thinkers—almost everyone else—didn't like to admit they'd been wrong.

Isaac Newton explained gravity. He said gravity is a force of nature that works at a distance and keeps the moon orbiting the earth—and he proved it mathematically. That idea set off explosions in the minds of thinking people. Suddenly it made sense to ask questions, look for evidence, and seek answers: in other words, to use the scientific method.

Newton was 82 when our good friend Ben Franklin first visited England at age 18. London was buzzing with new ideas. Ben dove into science head first. He studied the course of the Gulf Stream and its warmth, and figured out that ships' captains could follow it by using a thermometer. He examined colors and learned that they absorb heat at different rates. He discovered that electricity, like gravity, is one of nature's forces; that electricity has positive and negative charges; and that lightning is a form of electricity. All these were new concepts and disturbing to some people. Ben took a lot of abuse for his "ungodly" experiments with lightning.

It was a very old tradition to ring church bells during thunderstorms. That was supposed to ward off evil spirits. But a book published in 1784 noted that in the previous 35 years, lightning had struck 386 German churches and killed 103 bell ringers—making church-bell ringing a very hazardous occupation.

Ben Franklin devised lightning rods and put them on buildings—and they worked. They made those bolts harmless by conducting them into the ground. But when an earthquake struck Boston, Ben got blamed. It was said that his rods stole lightning from the skies and drained it into the earth, where it later exploded. (Not true, but it sounded likely.)

A French priest attacked Franklin, saying it was impertinent to guard against the "thunders of heaven." Ben answered, "Surely the Thunder of Heaven is no more Supernatural than the Rain, Hail or Sunshine of Heaven, against…which we guard by Roofs and Shades."

There's a point to all this. Science makes you think. And when you begin to think about the rules of nature, you go on to think about the rules of society. When Ben was a young businessman, he went along with common practices. He owned slaves. Later, when he got to thinking and working in science, he began to change his ideas on slavery. You can trace that change—step by step. In middle age he became a leader in the antislavery movement. As an old man, he introduced a bill in Congress calling for an end to slavery throughout the new nation. Congress didn't pass it.

As always, Franklin was way ahead of most others.

When people ask me who my favorite American is, I have a hard time answering—we have a passel of amazing national ancestors. This book is filled with them: people like Roger Williams and William Penn and Anne Hutchinson. But it is hard to do better than Benjamin Franklin. Besides all that impressive thinking, he was generous-spirited and a whole lot of fun. In the next book you will read more about him.

ATLAS
Atlas's Burden, or How The Atlas Got Its Name

You've heard the term "Earth-shaking." Well, this battle really shook the Earth. It was the Titans vs. Olympians. The Titans were led by Cronus, ruler of the Universe. The Olympians, who lived on Mt. Olympus, were led by Cronus's son, Zeus. Cronus was the supreme god but feared a takeover. (It had been predicted that one of his offspring would replace him.) So Cronus ate all his children, except baby Zeus who got hidden by his mother.

Zeus wanted to be the supreme god. First he tricked his father into upchucking his brothers and sisters (those Cronus had gulped down). Then Zeus got the hundred-handed giants on his side, along with the huge one-eyed Cyclopes (SIGH klow peas), who were master metalsmiths. The Cyclopes forged a helmet of darkness for Hades (Olympian ruler of the underworld), a trident for Poseidon (Olympian ruler of the seas), and thunderbolts for Zeus. Then the fight began.

Cronus's Titans weren't pushovers. They were gigantic. As I mentioned, the Earth shook when they battled. But Zeus and the crafty Olympians won. Having won, Zeus decided to punish the vanquished. He condemned Atlas, a muscular Titan, to hold the sky on his shoulders—forever.

Now this is the mythical story the Greeks told to explain why the sky doesn't fall. It has some other details that are interesting, so you might want to see if you can read more about it. (The Greek myths are among the best stories in the world.) Atlas also came to be identified with the Atlas Mountains in northwest Africa, which extend from Morocco to Algeria to Tunisia and often seem to be holding up the sky. (They were uplifted out of the Earth at the same time as the Alps Mountains in Europe and the Canary Islands to the west. That was in the late Jurassic Age.)

But how did Atlas's name get put on map books?

It was Gerhardus Mercator, who, without meaning to, named map books "atlases." In 1595, Mercator published a book of maps with a picture of muscular Atlas on the cover. Lots of people bought the book (Gutenberg had made that possible, and Mercator was one of the most skilled and influential mapmakers ever). Because of the cover picture, Mercator's book was soon known as "the atlas"; before long, other books of maps had that title.

The next pages include a mini- atlas for you to use as you read this history, or just for your own information. Maps tell stories and answer questions, I hope you enjoy these.

AR

Greenland

BAFFIN BAY

Iceland

Alaska
(U.S.)

HUDSON BAY

Ireland

United Kingdom

Canada

Portugal Spain Fr

United States

ATLANTIC OCEAN

Morocco

Bermuda

TROPIC of CANCER

Western Sahara

Alg

Hawaii
(U.S.)

GULF
of
MEXICO

Bahamas

Mexico

Cuba   Haiti
Dominican Republic
Puerto Rico

Mauritania

Mali

PACIFIC OCEAN

Belize
Honduras   Jamaica
CARIBBEAN SEA

Senegal
Cape Verde

Burkina
Faso

Guatemala
El Salvador   Nicaragua

Gambia
Guinea-Bissau
Guinea

Cote
d'Ivoire

Costa Rica

Cook Islands

Panama

Venezuela   Guyana
Suriname
French Guiana

Sierra Leone
Liberia

Togo
Be

Galapagos Is.
(Ecuador)

Colombia

Ghana

Kiribati

Ecuador

EQUATOR

Sao Tome & Principe
Equatorial G

Samoa

Brazil

American
Samoa

Peru

Tonga

Bolivia

Paraguay

TROPIC of CAPRICORN

Chile

Central Europe

0   100 Miles   0   100 Kilometers

Estonia

Russia

Denmark   Sweden

Latvia

Lithuania

Russia

Netherlands

Belarus

Germany

Poland

Belgium
Luxembourg

Czech
Republic

Ukraine

France

Austria   Slovakia

Moldova

Switzerland

Slovenia

Hungary

Italy

Croatia

Bosnia
&
Montenegro

Romania

San
Marino

Serbia
&

Monaco

Vatican
City

Macedonia

Bulgaria

Albania

Greece   Turkey

Argentina

Uruguay

Falkland Islands

East Caribbean

0   100 M.   0   100 K.

Saint Kitts
& Nevis

Antigua
& Barbuda

Montserrat

Guadeloupe

Dominica

Martinique

Saint Lucia

Saint Vincent and
the Grenadines

Barbad

Grenada

Trinidad
and
Tobago

Venezuela

A N T A R C T I C A

OCEAN

Finland

Russia

Belarus
Ukraine

Romania

Georgia
Armenia
Turkey
Cyprus
Syria
Lebanon
Israel
Jordan
Iraq
Iran
Kuwait
Egypt
Saudi Arabia
Qatar
Bahrain
United Arab
Emirates
Oman
Yemen
Eritrea
Djibouti

Kazakhstan

Uzbekistan
Turkmenistan
Azerbaijan

Afghanistan
Pakistan

Kyrgyzstan
Tajikistan

Mongolia

China

Nepal
Bhutan

India

N SEA

ARABIAN SEA

BAY
of
BENGAL

Bangladesh
Myanmar
(Burma)
Laos
Thailand

Sri Lanka

Maldives

Chad
Sudan

Central African
Republic
Ethiopia

Democratic
Republic
of the
Congo
Kenya
Tanzania
Burundi
Rwanda

Malawi
Comoros

Seychelles

INDIAN OCEAN

ola
Zambia
Zim-
babwe
Mozambique
Madagascar

Botswana

Reunion
Mauritius

South
Africa
Swaziland
Lesotho

Uganda
Somalia

North Korea
South Korea

Japan

Taiwan

Hong
Kong

Vietnam

Cambodia
Brunei
Malaysia

Singapore

Indonesia

BERING SEA

Philippines

Guam

PACIFIC OCEAN

PHILIPPINE SEA
Palau

Micronesia

Marshall Islands

Nauru

Tuvalu

Papua New
Guinea

Solomon Islands

CORAL SEA

Vanuatu

Fiji

New Caledonia

Australia

New Zealand

WORLD: POLITICAL

North America

South America

Europe

Asia

Africa

Australia & Oceania

N

W · E

S

Scale at the Equator.

Miles
0   1000   2000   3000

Kilometers
0   1000   2000   3000

CANADA

T

WASHINGTON

OREGON COUNTRY
Treaty with Great Britain
1846

OREGON

IDAHO

Missouri River

Red Riv

MONTANA

NORTH
DAKOTA

SOUTH
DAKOTA

WYOMING

THE LOUISIANA PU
From France
1803

Platte NEBRASKA
River

CEDED BY MEXICO
1845

NEVADA

UTAH

Colorado River

COLORADO

KANS

CALIFORNIA

Arkansas Rive

Canadian River

ARIZONA

NEW MEXICO

TEXAS

OK

Re

GADSDEN
PURCHASE
From Mexico 1853

TEXAS
Independent Repr
1836

Colora
Annexed
1845

PACIFIC

OCEAN

50°N

40°N

30°N

Annexed:
1898

20° N

HAWAII

0   300 Miles
0   300 Kilometers

160°W   155°W

160°W   140° W

70° N

RUSSIA

From
Russia
1867

CANADA

ALASKA

0   500 Miles
0   500 Kilometers

GULF OF CALIFORNIA

PUERTO RICO
Acquired
from Spain
1898

VIRGIN IS.
Acquired
from Denmark
1916-1917

PUERTO RICO

18N°

67°W   65°W

0   50 Miles

MEXICO

Rio Grande

N

W   E

S

120°W

100°W

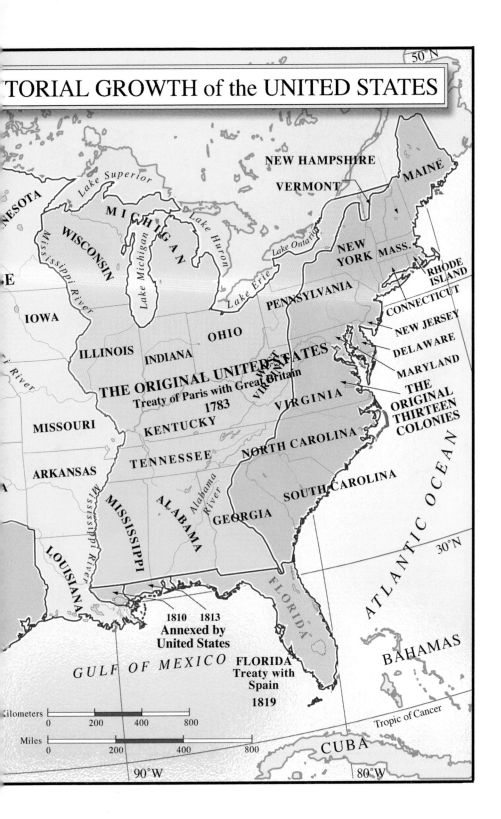

TORIAL GROWTH of the UNITED STATES

50°N

NEW HAMPSHIRE

VERMONT

MAINE

Lake Superior

MICHIGAN

Lake Huron

WISCONSIN

Lake Michigan

NESOTA

Mississippi River

Lake Ontario

NEW YORK

MASS.

RHODE ISLAND

E

Lake Erie

PENNSYLVANIA

CONNECTICUT

IOWA

NEW JERSEY

OHIO

DELAWARE

ILLINOIS

INDIANA

WEST VIRGINIA

MARYLAND

i River

THE ORIGINAL UNITED STATES

Treaty of Paris with Great Britain

1783

VIRGINIA

THE ORIGINAL THIRTEEN COLONIES

MISSOURI

KENTUCKY

NORTH CAROLINA

TENNESSEE

ARKANSAS

Alabama River

SOUTH CAROLINA

A

MISSISSIPPI

ALABAMA

GEORGIA

ATLANTIC OCEAN

30°N

LOUISIANA

Mississippi River

FLORIDA

1810   1813

Annexed by United States

BAHAMAS

GULF OF MEXICO

FLORIDA
Treaty with
Spain
1819

Kilometers

0   200   400   800

Tropic of Cancer

Miles

0   200   400   800

CUBA

90°W

80°W

Forest

Woodland (or used for farming)

Grassland (or used for farming or ranching)

184

RESOURCES, 1730

Whale

Bear

Deer & Elk

Buffalo

Fur

Horse

Turkey

Salt-water fish

Fresh-water fish

Obsidian & Flint

Timber

Iron

Water power

Lake Superior

Lake Michigan

Lake Huron

Lake Ontario

Lake Erie

ATLANTIC OCEAN

50°N

40°N

30°N

GULF OF MEXICO

BAHAMAS

Tropic of Cancer

CUBA

90°W

80°W

200 400 800

200 400 800

Brush (or used for ranching)

Desert

Tundra

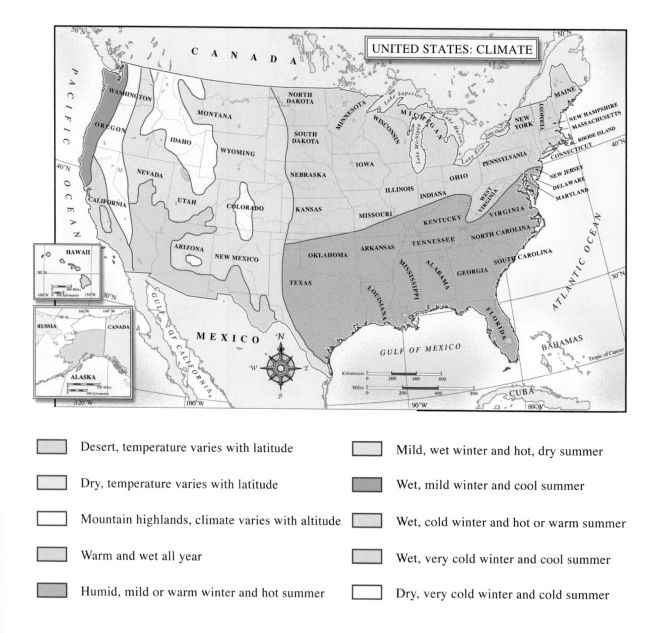

UNITED STATES: CLIMATE

Desert, temperature varies with latitude

Dry, temperature varies with latitude

Mountain highlands, climate varies with altitude

Warm and wet all year

Humid, mild or warm winter and hot summer

Mild, wet winter and hot, dry summer

Wet, mild winter and cool summer

Wet, cold winter and hot or warm summer

Wet, very cold winter and cool summer

Dry, very cold winter and cold summer